the study of
SOCIOLOGY

the study of
SOCIOLOGY

Caroline B. Rose

Department of Sociology
University of Minnesota

Arnold M. Rose, *Consultant*

Department of Sociology
University of Minnesota

CHARLES E. MERRILL BOOKS, INC., Columbus, Ohio

Library of Congress Catalog Card Number: 66–23545

3 4 5 6 7 8 9 10 11 12 13 14 15-76 75 74 73 72 71 70 69 68 67

Printed in the United States of America

Preface

There are several justifications for compressing the entire matter of sociology into one thin book. Compared to the physical and biological sciences, sociology is new, and many educated people have not studied it. As most young sciences do, sociology has been developing with great rapidity. New theories, techniques and applications occur yearly, so that sociological knowledge can become outdated in a short time. The practical applications of sociology in education, industry, medicine, and community organization have proved to be extremely useful to persons not trained primarily in the social sciences.

For all of these reasons, it has seemed worth while to provide a broad picture of the discipline for those who have not yet made the acquaintance of sociology and for those who would like a quick review of recent developments in the field. *The Study of Sociology* covers the assumptions, theories, methods and research findings of sociology and is written in a simple, easy-to-understand style with a non-technical vocabulary. This volume provides an interesting and accurate introduction to the fast-growing and important science of sociology.

Caroline B. Rose
Minneapolis, Minnesota

Contents

The Nature of Sociology

chapter one

SOCIOLOGY IS THE STUDY OF GROUP LIFE

Men everywhere live in groups. This is fortunate for sociologists because the consequences of group living are the subject matter of sociology. Their interest in groups is what distinguishes sociologists from other scientists. Among other things, sociologists want to know why groups like the family, the tribe, or the nation persist over time even during war or revolution. Why does a soldier fight and face death when he might hide or run away? Why does a man marry and take on responsibilities for a family when he might just as easily satisfy his sexual impulses outside of marriage? What effects does group living have on the behavior of group members? Do people who live in isolated, preliterate tribes behave differently from those who live in New York or a Parisian suburb? Are the attitudes of a slum dweller different from those of an upper-class businessman and, if so, why?

Sociologists are equally interested in why groups change or fall apart. For example, they want to know why some marriages end in divorce. They are interested in why there is more divorce in some countries than there is in others and why the rates of divorce increase or decrease over time. They want to know if people behave differently after they move from the country to the city or from the city to the suburbs.

Finally, sociologists study the relationships among group members and among groups. What are the relationships between husband and wife and between parents and children in the United States today? Are these relationships like those in the early American family or like those in families in other countries? What

1

causes conflict between Negroes and whites in the South? Do labor, industry, and government in the United States relate to each other in the same way as do similar groups in Australia or the Soviet Union? Why do some groups in the society have more material goods and more prestige than do others?

SOCIOLOGY IS ONE OF A GROUP OF SOCIAL SCIENCES

Sociology is a science, and sociologists, like all other scientists, try to explain the phenomena within their field and to test their explanations. Anthropology, economics, political science, history, and geography are the other social sciences, and with each of them sociology has many common interests.

Anthropology and sociology are specialized branches of the same science. Anthropologists have usually studied preliterate or nonindustrialized societies, and sociologists have concentrated on the study of complex, modern, industrial societies. Each science has invented research techniques suited to study the kinds of groups in which it is interested. Both sociology and anthropology examine group or social behavior. Or, as it may be alternately stated, both sciences study man's culture. The basic theory in both sciences is the same.

Certain kinds of human behavior are studied by both sociologists and economists. For example, institutional economists and sociologists are interested in how and why labor unions develop the way they do and in their relationship to other groups in the society. Both are concerned with the types of personality that develop and predominate in a capitalist society, where competition is an important value.

Similarly, sociologists and political scientists are often interested in the same phenomena. The study of public opinion is of equal interest to them. So is voting behavior or the structure of political parties.

For a description of any social act that does not occur within immediate experience, sociologists are dependent upon historians to tell them what occurred. When historians are wrong, sociological theory will be wrong. In 1935 W. E. B. Du Bois, a famous historian, published a book called *Black Reconstruction*. It became evident that if the facts in *Black Reconstruction* were correct (they were heavily documented and are generally accepted by both historians and sociologists today), then the facts previously presented about the history of the Negro in the United States could not be true. Among other things, Du Bois stated that the Negroes elected to

Congress from the South and to Southern state legislatures during the Reconstruction Period after the Civil War were an educated group and that the legislation they enacted was sober, intelligent, and progressive. Negro legislators were not field hands, right out of the cotton fields, ordering gold spittoons for the state houses, as historians had reported. Sociologists then had to discard their theory that a large part of the antagonism between whites and Negroes in the South was the result of lack of education and irresponsible legislation on the part of Negro representatives during Reconstruction.

The relationship between sociology and geography is complex. American geographers have not traditionally been interested in examining the effects of the physical environment on the inter-relationships among men, although European geographers have. What changes in social life occur when the city is extended out-ward by the invention of mass transportation? In what kinds of city neighborhoods is there juvenile delinquency? When a neigh-borhood begins to change from residential to commercial, what happens to the families living there? To examine these and similar questions neglected by geographers, a special science, human ecology, arose within sociology. Today, ecology is a separate science, taught in departments of sociology, geography, and, some-times, economics. Ecologists know a great deal about how a city changes and grows, and it is unfortunate that they are not asked for practical advice more often. They could point out to city planners, for example, that a device to raise land values in the blighted areas in our core cities would improve the character of the areas in a short time and would save the money and red tape involved in laboriously trying to reconstruct these areas. Ecologists also have a great deal of information about how transit routes develop and their relationships to the distribution of people. If this knowledge were used in laying out freeway routes, city administrators would be more successful in reducing urban sprawl and stopping the flight of people and money from the cities to the suburbs.

Psychology is the study of individual behavior and is not considered a social science. There is, however, a close relationship between one of the subdivisions of psychology—social psychology—and one of the basic fields of sociology, also called social psychology. There is enough difference between the theoretical orientation of social psychologists trained in psychology and those trained in sociology that when both groups mutually attack a problem both gain, as the following example illustrates.

Social psychologists are interested in personality, which they define as the patterned or typical ways in which an individual relates himself to the world and to other individuals. Else Frenkel-Brunswik and her associates, psychologists with a Freudian background, found that individuals with strong anti-Semitic attitudes also had anti-Negro attitudes and were rigid, compulsive, and overconforming in their personalities. They called this personality type "the authoritarian personality."

Sociologists were much interested in these findings because they confirmed and gave an explanation for the results of *social distance* [1] tests which showed that highly prejudiced individuals would extend their prejudices even to imaginary groups. Sociologists raised some further questions. Do some kinds of families or some kinds of child-raising habits produce more authoritarian personalities than do others? Since the individual with an authoritarian personality overconforms, he must be conforming to a society which values prejudice. If the society values equality, the overconforming individual should overvalue equality. Is there, then, a differential value on prejudice in different parts of the society? Subsequent research by both psychologists and sociologists seems to show that some lower-class families in the United States do produce more individuals with authoritarian personalities. Since the same group tends to value prejudice, this explains why anti-Semitism and anti-Negro feelings are closely associated with this personality type.

SOCIOLOGY IS DIVIDED INTO SEVERAL SUBFIELDS

The two main theoretical fields of sociology are Social Organization and Social Psychology.

Social Organization or Social Structure

As might be expected in a science which studies group behavior, sociologists, working in one of its two central fields, are preoccupied with classifying and analyzing the structure of groups and studying the relations among them. Although incomplete, for reasons of space, the following list suggests the kinds of groups and relationships and some of their characteristics that interest sociologists:

1. *Institutions:* relatively permanent groups present in almost all societies, like the family, the army, a school, or an industry.

---

[1] See p. 31.

2. *Small, voluntary groups:* groups more ephemeral than institutions; found in some societies much more than in others, like the PTA's, delinquent gangs, bridge clubs, political parties.
3. *Stratified groups:* groups, like castes and classes, whose members have differential amounts of whatever the society values and which, as a result, have differential amounts of power.
4. *Relationships within and among groups:* relationships such as conflict within a political party or between political parties, or the accommodation that results when union and industry representatives sign a contract.
5. *Relationships within and among groups as they are affected by the environment:* as the effect of a rural or suburban environment on the family or the school system.

Having said that sociologists are interested in groups, the writer must immediately qualify this statement. To the layman, "the family" probably calls up a picture of mother, father, and two children setting off together for a picnic or to church. A sociologist will mentally translate "the family" into another phrase, "a cluster of interrelated roles." To the layman this is gibberish. To the sociologist it is clarification. As a radiologist is interested not in the skin and flesh that clothe the body but in the internal structure his X rays reveal, so the sociologist is not interested in the concrete manifestations of family life, but in reaching, with his conceptual tools, what it is in the family that is "social."

Probably everybody today is aware that to a physicist a table is not a solid, substantial support for the dinner one eats off it, but a whirling mass of billions of electrified particles, moving in regular and recurrent patterns. Every educated person grants the physicist the right to look at the dining room table in this way and understands that he is concerned with basic units and processes which explain the structure of all matter and not just the matter of the dining room table. In exactly the same way the sociologist seeks basic social units and processes whose properties and relations explain group behavior in general.

In some groups, like the family or the army, the members mutually adjust their behavior by communicating and interacting. with each other. From the point of view of how group members relate to each other, the family and the army, although superficially dissimilar, are basically the same. In sociological jargon, they are *integrated groups.* An integrated group is one of the basic units sociologists work with. *Social processes* are other basic sociological units. Within a family, there is often conflict—among siblings, for example. Within the larger society, conflict occurs between labor and business or among political parties. Sociologists have discovered that conflict is a social process that can be studied in and of itself no matter where it occurs. What is learned about the causes of conflict and its resolution in the family can be applied equally precisely to political conflict.

Social Psychology

One of the subdivisions of the second important theoretical field of sociology, social psychology, is called *collective behavior*— the study of the behavior of individuals in *nonintegrated groups*. *Crowds, audiences,* and *publics* are examples of nonintegrated groups, and their distinguishing characteristic is that their members do not communicate with one another.

The primary concern of social psychology, however, has to do with how the individual and the group are related. A baby is an animal with only the potentialities of becoming a human being. If a baby is deprived of contact with human beings it does not become human, as studies of abandoned, neglected, rejected, or isolated, but mentally normal, children show. An adult deprived of human contact will cease to exhibit human traits. An individual who is mentally ill is either totally or in part nonhuman, depending on the severity of his illness. These are the most basic and best substantiated facts in sociology, and they apply everywhere in the world.

What is it that makes human beings human? Obviously, it cannot be something that grows spontaneously and inevitably in the individual since it develops only when the individual is in a group. It must be something that joins the individual to other members of a group, but just as obviously it is not something concrete and visible like a bridge which joins an island to the mainland.

To answer these questions, social psychologists postulate (that is, invent and name) a quality in the individual which can be developed only by communication and interaction with other group members. This quality they call the *social self*. The ways in which this self is developed they call *socialization*. The social self is not tangible. It is not located in the liver or the brain. It is not synonymous with the concept of personality mentioned a few pages back. It is much less than the total individual. One of the main tasks of social psychologists is to give form and shape to this elusive abstraction, the social self, and to explain its genesis and development.

History of Sociology

In order to avoid the mistakes of their predecessors, sociologists study the history of their science. An interesting and fruitful subdivision of this field is the *sociology of knowledge*. Law; science; literature and the other arts; and political, economic, and religious ideologies are all products of group life and can, therefore, be studied in the same way as can other products of group life. With the same techniques one uses to study why the child-rearing techniques of American middle-class families have become "permissive," one can also study why American sociologists of the thirties were preoccupied with social change in contrast to sociologists in the sixties, who are more concerned with consensus or agreement in society.

Social Problems

Individuals frequently enter sociology because they are interested in social problems and want to find solutions for them.[2] The field of social problems has always been a large and lively one, but its content has undergone much change. Crime is always with us; one of the few enduring divisions within the field of social problems is *criminology*. *Medical sociology* is new. Among other things, medical sociologists study the problems of administering large institutions; the relations among the medical professions and between the medical professions and their clienteles; and institutional arrangements that have therapeutic value for both physical and mental disorders. At one time *immigration* was a major interest of sociologists. Today, it is of little concern, but the study of *minority group relations* is important.

Sometimes the study of a social problem starts for a reason which becomes less important as the field grows. *Industrial sociology* was stimulated immediately after World War I by a few large industries interested in weaning workers away from unions. Industrial sociologists today are hired by, and study, unions as well as industries, and the field includes the study of any kind of group behavior within the industrial sector of a society.

---

[2] This statement does not imply that sociologists as a group have any obligation to try to solve social problems. Their commitment is to develop the science of sociology. Whether or not one works in the field of social problems is a matter of taste and interest.

Changes in the content of the field mirror changes in the society. When a problem is solved, or when a society is not interested in solving the problem, sociologists generally do not study it. This is not only because sociologists reflect the concerns of the society of which they are a part but also because sociological research is expensive. Only when society regards a situation as both undesirable and susceptible to change is there enough money and institutional support to pursue the study of the problem adequately.

The field of social problems should not be regarded as parallel to the fields of social structure and social psychology. It is, rather, a large laboratory in which the basic theory of sociology is developed, tested, and applied. Medicine could not have found the cause and cure of polio by studying only its symptoms. It was necessary to study epidemiology, virology, and serology. Similarly, juvenile vandalism or race riots are symptoms of social problems, and to understand and cure them it is necessary to study social structure and social psychology. A large part of sociological theory has been developed by studying social problems, just as knowledge of the nature of viruses was increased by studying polio. There have always been some sociologists who deprecate the study of social problems and advise sociologists to concentrate on "pure" research. They say that only when basic theory is completely understood will we have enough knowledge to solve social problems. This is perhaps like trying to find the causes of polio without ever seeing a polio patient!

Population or Demography

The study of the growth and distribution of human populations (*population* or *demography*) is a separate science which historically has been taught in departments of sociology in the United States. Demography becomes important to sociologists when they study the kind of problem discussed below.

Since World War II the average life expectancy of people reaching the age of sixty has been extended by various medical advances. What does it mean to the individual who lives long past this age in a society which is not prepared to take care of him? This is one of the questions which interest sociologists. Before they could begin to analyze the effects of an increase in the aged, sociologists would need to know how many people of each sex there are in the over-sixty age group; how much income and education they have; what religion they profess; where they live; what proportion of the total population they represent; and how these factors have changed over a given time span. It takes special techniques to collect these data accurately, and sociologists turn to demographers for them.

METHODS OF RESEARCH

All sociologists must understand research methodology. Some sociologists devote the bulk of their time to developing and testing new research instruments and processes. Because of its importance, Chapter 3 is devoted entirely to *methodology*.

In these few pages, I have tried to indicate the kinds of situations and events that arouse the curiosity of sociologists and stimulate them to speculation and research. The careful reader should also have become aware that sociologists have their own "perspective"; that is, when they are acting as sociologists, they view the world in a specialized way. The next chapter tells of the development of sociology and will try to show how this peculiar perspective developed.

Some Important Developments in Sociology   chapter two

THE INTERNATIONAL CHARACTER OF SOCIOLOGY

Sociology received its name and its purpose—the scientific study of society—from a Frenchman, Auguste Comte (1798–1847). The name, however, preceded the fact, and sociology could not be regarded as a science until sociologists were able to define a field of study and to devise empirical methods to investigate it. Sociology emerged at the end of the nineteenth century almost simultaneously in Europe (in France, Germany, and Italy) and in the United States. During this period many American sociologists completed their education in Europe. They brought home the theories of the great French sociologists, Emile Durkheim (1855–1917) Gabriel Tarde (1843–1904) and Gustav Le Bon (1841–1931); and, from Germany, the theories of Max Weber (1864–1920) and Georg Simmel (1858–1918). Thus, from the very beginning sociology has had an international character.

Despite its auspicious beginning, sociology in Europe has developed in an inconsistent fashion. Only in France has sociology had both an early start and continual growth, resulting today in chairs in all the leading universities, a rich variety of sociological schools and theoretical approaches, and a brilliant roster of names. German sociology, one of the most fruitful in the world, was destroyed by Hitler. There is now only a feeble development in Germany. A flourishing school of sociology in Italy was seriously weakened under Fascism and is just beginning to revive. There

10

was a small development in Finland, started by E. A. Westermarck (1862–1939), and another in Poland, originating in the work of Florian Znaniecki (1882–1958). Poland has managed to maintain its sociological traditions through war and dictatorships, something other countries in a similar position have been unable to do.

In 1949 UNESCO stimulated and provided financial support for a meeting in Oslo to found the *International Sociological Association* (ISA). The first full-fledged meeting of the ISA was held in Zurich in 1950 and was attended by 100 delegates from a score of countries. Since that time, meetings have been held at regular intervals. The latest—the 1962 session in Washington, D.C.—was attended by over 1,000 delegates. This figure alone indicates the significant expansion of sociology in only twelve years.

In addition to the assistance, stimulation, and inspiration scholars receive from each other, international communication among sociologists is important in a more direct way to the future of this field. Sociologists hope to find universal laws of human behavior. Some sociologists hold that this is impossible because most human behavior is culture-bound. Until now there has been little opportunity for sociologists—unlike anthropologists—to do the comparative studies that would furnish proof on one side or the other. The programs of the ISA are always centered around a main subject and are announced three years ahead of time. This encourages sociologists from different countries to concentrate their research in the field which will be examined at the next international meeting. As a result, the *Proceedings of the World Congresses* provide a series of comparative studies about modern society never before available.

Sociology is now studied in all European countries except, perhaps, Portugal and Albania. Japan, Israel, Egypt, Turkey, and India have a number of sociologists; and the work in Japan and Israel is often first rate. Sociological study is going on in South and Central American countries, and Brazil and Mexico have some strength in the field. The leading political opponent of Prime Minister Nkrumah in Ghana was K. A. Busia, an English-trained sociologist, now in exile. Sociology is beginning in New Zealand and Australia.

It is a tribute to the accomplishments of American sociologists that sociology has been called "the American science." As the preceding paragraphs show, this is an exaggeration, but sociology has developed more rapidly in the United States than elsewhere. Students and professors have traveled back and forth between Canadian and American universities to study and teach.

Thus, sociology in Canada has developed simultaneously and co-operatively with that in the United States.

THE ABANDONMENT OF SINGLE-CAUSE, DETERMINIST THEORIES OF SOCIAL BEHAVIOR

Such a capsule history does not reveal how sociology moved from a wish to study society to a science capable of explaining a great deal about social life. What follows is a description of some of the important discoveries that shaped modern sociology.

A striking trend in sociology has been the progressive abandonment of monistic (one-cause), determinist theories of social behavior. These theories assume that social behavior is shaped and controlled by one powerful and impersonal force, like heredity or economic conditions or culture.

In the late nineteenth and early twentieth centuries, biology, particularly in the field of genetics, made spectacular strides. The excitement engendered by these advances permeated all intellectual life, and many sociologists were seduced into attributing variations in social behavior to hereditary differences. Lombroso and his followers believed that criminals inherited their "criminal nature" and that they could be distinguished from other people by the size of their heads or the shape of their ear lobes. Others believed that mental illness was inherited. In the United States anti-immigration laws were supported by statements of sociologists that some national groups were so different in heredity from the population already here that they could never be assimilated. These arguments, used first against the Chinese and next against the Irish, were applied to each successive wave of immigrants—the Scandinavians, Central Europeans, and, finally, the Italians. The same arguments were used to oppose labor legislation and slum clearance. The lower classes, it was said, were biologically inferior, and no legal changes could improve their condition.[1]

Other sociologists refuted biological determinism. They pointed out that the heredity make-up of a population is constant, whereas social behavior changes rapidly. For example: criminals reform,

---

[1] One of the most notorious studies of this kind compares two family histories—that of the Jukes and that of the Kallikaks. The Jukes supposedly exhibited every possible kind of moral and social deviation generation after generation, while the Kallikaks were all model citizens. Later investigators found that practically none of the family members had been interviewed or traced to the original progenitors. This study is mentioned because it is still often found in outdated secondary texts.

the mentally ill recover, the children of illiterate immigrants become doctors and lawyers, and the lower classes move rapidly into the middle class. Studies of criminals showed that, as a group, they did not differ from the noncriminal population in appearance, intelligence, or temperament.

Although biological or hereditary determinism has no scientific standing whatsoever today, it is still accepted among laymen, particularly in the form of racism. The same kind of empirical evidence that destroyed the credibility of biological determinism as a cause of criminality is available to disprove various aspects of racism. For example: Southern Negro children who migrate North exhibit an increase in their I.Q. scores. Northern-educated Negroes score higher on army intelligence tests, on the average, than do Southern-educated whites. There are many cases of Negro children with high I.Q.'s, some as high as 200. None of these things would be possible if intelligence were linked with race. Many other studies could be cited to show that no racial group has a monopoly on any kind of social behavior, good or bad.[2]

As research demonstrated fallacies in biological determinism, many social scientists began to attribute the causes of social behavior entirely to the influence of the environment, particularly the economic environment. Economic determinism springs from the ideas of Karl Marx and is widely accepted, although many businessmen would blanch upon being told that some of their theories of social behavior bear a resemblance to Marxist theories. The belief that a capitalistic economic system can solve all problems is as much economic determinism as the persuasion that socialism will cure all the world's ills. Some sociologists, particularly in Europe, analyzed society in Marxist terms. Others developed more specific and narrower theories.

In 1929 William Fielding Ogburn (1886–1959) was asked by President Hoover to direct a study of social change. Published under the title of *Recent Social Trends* (1930–1933), the study provides a wealth of accurate, statistical information about the United States in the period following World War I, but its theory

---

[2] For refutations of biological determinism, see: Charles Horton Cooley, "Genius, Fame and the Comparison of Race," *Annals of the American Academy of Political and Social Science*, IX (May 1897), 317–58; Franz Boas, *The Mind of Primitive Man* (New York: The Macmillan Co., 1911); Abraham Myerson, *The Inheritance of Mental Diseases* (Baltimore: The Williams & Wilkins Co., 1925); Otto Klineberg, *Race Differences* (New York: Harper & Row, Publishers, 1935). Notice the dates on these references; they were deliberately chosen to show how long it sometimes takes for a theory to die even after it is scientifically refuted.

is an example of economic determinism. Ogburn pivoted the study around the idea that, although technological change is constantly occurring, in an industrial society there is often a lag between technological change and the adaptation of society to the new technology—i.e., a *culture lag.*

Causal explanations of this sort are still common. One hears over and over that automation is causing unemployment. If this is so, why is it that in the USSR and other European countries automation does not cause unemployment? In Russia if an industry is automated the government shifts the displaced labor to another sector of the economy—something our belief in individual freedom prevents our government from doing. In many European countries, the government manipulates the economy to provide a slight inflation to stimulate industrial expansion and absorb excess labor. Similar solutions have been slow of acceptance in the United States. Until recently, technological unemployment fell most heavily on minority groups. Relatively few citizens have cared enough to accept the higher taxes necessary to retrain minority group workers. The cause of unemployment in an increasingly auto-mated society, then, is not the oversimplified culture lag, but a complicated interplay of American attitudes toward government, economics, and race.

Formerly, economic determinism was accepted as the cause of the class structure of our society and as the reason for discrimi-nation against minority groups. Research has shown the causes of both phenomena to be more complex. At one time it was assumed that broken homes, poverty, and disorganized neighborhoods (used as indices of economic factors) were responsible for juvenile delinquency, illegitimacy, adult crimes, unemployability, the prob-lems of old age, and even mental deficiency and mental illness. When, however, studies showed that many individuals subject to these influences did not exhibit problem behavior and that many of those who did misbehave came from economically satisfactory backgrounds, the economic determinist theories were weakened.

Max Weber, a German sociologist, was highly influential in discrediting economic determinism. He did a series of monographs on the influence of religious ideas on the rest of social life, the best known of which is *The Protestant Ethic and The Spirit of Capitalism.* He showed that the rise of Protestantism (particularly Calvinism with its emphasis on individual rights and responsi-bilities) not only preceded modern European capitalism in time but provided an extremely congenial atmosphere for its growth. Weber's brilliant analysis of the effect of ideologies on the economic structure of societies played an important part in turning sociology away from economic determinism.

Monistic deterministic theories were also expressed in *social determinism* or *cultural determinism.* Social determinism has yielded some lasting concepts, although its point of view has been abandoned. The chief exponent of social determinism was William Graham Sumner (1840–1910), one of the earliest American sociologists. Sumner exemplifies a school of sociology called Social Darwinism, after Charles Darwin, creator of the theory of evolution. At one time this was a leading school of sociological thought, boasting such names as Herbert Spencer (1820–1903) in England and Lester Ward (1841–1913) in the United States.

The Folkways, Sumner's major work, is a study of *social control*—the ways in which a social group inculcates the values of the group into the minds of its members and prevents deviant behavior, producing common agreement or *consensus.* When social control and consensus break down, revolution and reorganization of the society occur. Nobody knows how much consensus a society needs to function, but this is one of the central concerns of sociologists today. Sumner thought of the operation of social control as automatic and inevitable and believed that the individual was completely formed and controlled by the operation of "natural" social laws. This is what is meant by social determinism.

Social determinism was not as easy to refute as biological and economic determinisms had been, but it, too, yielded to analysis. The following sections show how and why sociologists have finally abandoned all monistic, deterministic theories.

THE SEARCH FOR VALID GENERALIZATIONS

Sociologists have abandoned single-cause theories because they find that both the causes and effects of social behavior are very complex. For example, today many married women are going to work when their children are half grown. The involved myriad of events that precipitated the large-scale return of married women to work developed over a long period of time. The idea that women are not biologically inferior to men and should have equal political and economic rights has been gaining acceptance for a hundred years. This is an ideological factor. Another factor is the availability of methods to limit family size. The invention of birth control techniques is a technological change. Their acceptance is an ideological change. There are other causative factors such as the movement of large groups of people into the middle class so that a second salary becomes necessary to maintain the desired standard of living. Women have been freer to work outside the home since the invention of low-cost, processed foods and labor-saving devices for the home. This series of interrelated changes is certainly not the result of the working of any single, immutable, "natural" law— biological, economic, or cultural.

Many social institutions are being affected by the movement of married women into the labor force, and there will be effects in the future on which we can only speculate at this time. For example, many women are going into teaching because it has traditionally been a woman's profession and because the hours of work coincide with the hours when their children are away from home. An influx of mature married women into the teaching profession can affect both the teaching profession and the structure of the educational system. Mothers experienced in raising children may well challenge current educational theories and practice with an assurance younger trainees could not have. Teachers have traditionally submitted tamely to low wages and community control of their behavior, in part because most of them were single women entirely dependent on their salaries. Married women, whose earnings constitute a second family salary and whose community status is established, can afford to be more independent.

There have been predictions that when mothers work outside the home there will be an increase of divorce and juvenile delinquency. The evidence about an increase of divorce is unclear, but studies show that there is little relation between juvenile delinquency and the working mother.

As more women move into the labor force, we can expect an increase in the purchase of processed food and ready-made clothing, of labor-saving devices for the home, and of second family automobiles. Voluntary associations like the PTA, the Girl Scouts, the Red Cross, and political clubs are finding it more difficult to recruit leadership. The working woman does not have time for much volunteer activity.

Similarly any social event is both the result of a multiplicity of causes and itself a contributing cause to other social events. *In sociological terms all the institutions of a society and its culture are interrelated over time.* Sociologists are not only interested in the interrelationships among institutions. They are also concerned about how any change affects society as a whole. How, for example, do the changes in women's roles affect consensus?

At one time in the United States, there was consensus that a woman should stay at home and be a good wife and mother. Most people agreed on this, and there was little behavior deviating from this value. Today, some people disapprove of married women working. Others accept it. In certain circles women are being urged not to waste their talents and education on housework when they have no small children. There is thus much less consensus about the role of married women than there was fifty years ago. Different parts of the society are inculcating different values.

Is it possible to find a sociological generalization that will do justice to multiple causation, explain the interrelationships of institutions, and deal with society as a whole at the same time? Such generalizations are rare, but there are some.

The Theory of the Division of Labor

One of the generalizations or laws adequate to explain the complexity of society is the *division of labor*. In 1893 Emile Durkheim published *The Division of Labor in Society*, developing therein the division of labor concept which has proved useful in analyzing both *consensus* and *stratification*.

A modern industrial society is characterized by a multiplicity of occupational groups—teachers, doctors, shoemakers, public relations experts, civil servants, astronauts, garbage collectors, and others. Because the work of each group is specialized, everyone in the society is highly dependent upon everyone else. The society as a whole can continue only when each group carries out its occupational tasks. Mutual dependence of groups holds modern societies together (creates consensus).

On the other hand, the work one does leads to differences in income, education, prestige, and attitudes toward the world. Sociologists say that the society is *stratified*. Sometimes they call this kind of society *pluralistic*. Does the division of labor mean then that one's loyalties belong first to the occupational group and only secondly to the larger society? Is the mutual economic dependence of groups more compelling than the mutual antagonisms that develop out of different world views? When a labor union in a basic industry threatens to go on strike or a basic industry raises its prices, these questions assume practical importance. Exclusive loyalty to one's profession may also spring from the division of labor. Physicians in Belgium in April, 1964, angered at government regulation of their profession, went on strike and refused to treat any but the most critically ill. Eventually, the government had to draft doctors into the army to avoid complete panic and collapse of the society. Similarly, on the basis of the division of labor theory, we might ask what are the consequences for the society of confining one group to menial occupations, as has been done to Negroes in the United States?

In a pluralistic society, people are exposed to world views different from their own. Does this lead them to harden their own views? Does it make them more tolerant? Does it weaken every point of view so that none survives? If this happens, does the society collapse or does a new and common *ideology* (set of beliefs and values) emerge? These are questions of consensus for which sociologists are trying to find adequate answers. One approach is to examine in detail the ways in which a group inculcates and enforces group values on the group members (social control).

The Relationship Between the Individual and the Group

In the process of abandoning determinism of all kinds, sociologists learned that men's behavior is influenced at one and the same time by their biological structure, the functioning of their minds, the kind of culture they are a part of, their relations with others, their past experiences, the kinds of groups they participate in, and the particular circumstances of an act. Many sociologists began to conceive of men *acting within a social structure*. Their behavior is not determined; men choose their behavior. Herbert Blumer describes this point of view:

> Instead of the individual being surrounded by an environment of pre-existing objects which play upon him and call forth his behavior, the proper picture is that he constructs his objects on the basis of his on-going activity. . . . His behavior, accordingly, is not a result of such things as environmental pressures, stimuli, motives, attitudes and ideas, but arises instead from how he interprets and handles these things in the action which he is now constructing.[3]

When the construction of an action by an individual is analyzed further, the following facts emerge:

1. Each individual is unique.
2. Nevertheless, some individuals behave similarly. New Yorkers behave more like each other than they do like Romans. Most men act more like other men than like women.

---

[3] "Society as Symbolic Interaction," in Arnold M. Rose (ed.), *Human Behavior and Social Processes* (Boston: Houghton Mifflin Co., 1962), pp. 182–83.

3. Individuals occupying different positions in society behave differently, and individuals behave differently at different times. A business executive behaves differently than a coal miner. Both of them behave differently toward their children than they do to their co-workers or their ministers, although they may behave differently from each other in each of these relations.

4. Society is always changing. Each generation wonders what the next is coming to.

5. On the other hand, groups exhibit continuity. They have traditions that are passed on from generation to generation.

An adequate theory of social behavior must explain both change and stability, both unique and common behavior, and how individuals relate to the other members of the group. To account for individuality and uniqueness, sociologists postulate, as one part of the social self,[4] something they call the *I*. Like the self, the I does not really exist. It is a concept sociologists have invented. Common observation shows that no two individuals, even identical twins, behave exactly alike. No two women mother their children in exactly the same way, although they may agree entirely on how children should be raised. No two teachers teach in exactly the same manner, even though they have been teaching the same subject in the same school for the same length of time, have been professionally trained in the same department of education, and agree on what should be taught and how to teach it. Whatever it is within the self that constructs behavior uniquely for each individual (and we do not know what it is at present) is subsumed under the term, the I.

Similarly, in order to explain the fact that people frequently act alike, sociologists assume that the self contains reflections of what the group or society expects. These expectations are called *me's*. When the me's are related and cluster together, they are called *roles*. All the expectations society has of how women should behave constitute the role of women. As we have said earlier, people live in groups and they therefore learn, in a variety of ways, how other members of the group expect them to behave in certain circumstances. Each person internalizes (integrates into the self structure) the expectations of the groups he belongs to. This explains why members of the same group behave alike and why members of different groups behave differently. For example, it explains why teachers behave more like other teachers than they do like salesmen.

---

[4] See pp. 6–7.

Why have sociologists been concerned with mapping out the internal structure of the self? For one thing, they can thus explain why social control works. An individual will not respond to social controls, like gossip or prison or the awarding of public esteem, unless his social self contains the appropriate expectations or me's. Threats that the high-school drop-out will receive low wages or face unemployment will fall on deaf ears unless the student feels that steady employment and a high income are desirable.[5] A woman who belongs to a group that does not frown on illegitimacy, although most other groups in a society do, is likely to produce illegitimate children even though the larger society punishes her.

From the point of view of the larger society, anything which blocks the internalization of expectations for a large group of people is important to study. Isolation of a group, whatever its cause, results in the group members learning different kinds of expectations than most of us do. The Southerner who practices segregation today, the rural Negro male who does not fulfill his paternal role, the lower-class slum child who rejects what the school wants to teach him, many American Indian tribes who try to live as their ancestors did, the mentally ill—all of these groups behave in ways not consonant with the expectations of the majority of Americans. Their behavior can only be changed by directing proper expectations toward them in situations in which they can internalize the expectations. This requires knowing how social expectations are acquired—a process studied under the name of socialization.

Change, as well as isolation, can also result in a failure of social control. When a social catastrophe occurs—war or revolution or rapid social change resulting in unemployment—the individual finds that the behavior society once expected of him (which he has internalized or learned) is either no longer possible or does not bring social approval. When a man cannot find work, he may no longer be respected and looked up to by his family and neighbors. He knows society expects him to work. He wants to work but he cannot. He becomes bewildered, sometimes apathetic, sometimes mentally ill, and sometimes anti-social. Retired people are often in this situation because a lifetime of hard work has brought them neither economic security nor prestige. Social control fails because the fulfillment of social expectations is unrewarding. In a society whose population is increasing and enjoying a progressively higher standard of living and education, those who rise

---

[5] He may, of course, just not believe the threats will materialize, but that is a separate problem.

socially and economically may not have internalized the expectations relevant to their new situation. They may not know, for example, how to motivate their children to want a higher education. When a great many groups in a society find that the expectations directed toward them are impossible to fulfill or when they do not understand what the expectations are because of isolation or change, social controls fail and consensus breaks down.

This chapter has not been, in the main, a conventional history of sociology. By showing some of the false roads sociology has followed and then forsaken, the author has tried to help the reader avoid these unrewarding paths. It is hoped that the exposition of some of the complexities of social life has made clear why sociologists have created abstract and difficult concepts. Modern sociologists are face to face with the difficult task of studying very complex phenomena, parts of which are concealed inside the minds of individuals. This condition has affected not only their approach and the kind of concepts they invent, but also the way in which they interpret and apply scientific method. The next chapter will explore the methodology of sociology.

The Methods
Employed by chapter three
Sociologists

OBSTACLES TO SOCIOLOGICAL RESEARCH

The nature of the material social scientists study creates problems that natural scientists do not have. If an amoeba is unhappy about having its private life bared to the world, the biologist does not know this. If he did, he probably would not care. Social scientists are, however, restricted in their ability to observe all aspects of human behavior.

Sexual life is private. Many people are reluctant to reveal their financial status, police records, or other situations which shame and embarrass them. Even if an informant thinks he is answering a questionnaire truthfully, he may not be. Men have a great capacity for deceiving themselves. When a man's reasons for thinking or doing something lie in his unconscious mind, they are accessible to the researcher only by special techniques.

In our society a sociologist can experiment with human beings only to a limited degree and only with their permission. The use of cameras and recording devices without the knowledge or consent of the people being studied creates situations in which invasion of privacy and blackmail may result. Both psychologists and sociologists have recently attempted to formulate codes of ethics which forbid observing people without their prior permission. Knowledge of our own behavior tells us, however, that when people know they are being observed they are not likely to behave exactly as they would if they thought no one was about. Even the observation of public life is often restricted. When one sociologist, for example, wanted to place a recording machine in a jury room to find out how decisions were reached, the courts forbade it.

Finally, a social scientist studies creatures like himself. With some of them he may share experiences, attitudes, and values. Others may engage in behavior which he abhors. Like other men, the social scientist may not be completely aware of his own attitudes or know that some of them are determined in his unconscious.

In the face of all the peculiar circumstances that surround the study of society, sociologists have had to be sure that it was *possible* to have a science of social behavior. A part of every sociologist's professional training is a study of *what* conditions have to be met in order to have a science. He is also taught a variety of ways of preventing, or at least minimizing, the intrusion of his own values into his scientific studies.

HOW A SOCIOLOGIST DOES HIS WORK

It is often stated, and probably widely believed, that a scientist starts by observing the facts. A little reflection will show that this is impossible. Which facts? There are billions of facts in the world. Nobody can ever observe them all—certainly not a sociologist setting out to do a small piece of research in a limited area. The first thing a scientist has to do is to decide what he is going to study. The kind of scientist he is determines this in part. An endocrinologist is unlikely to be interested in volcanic structure. Similarly, a sociologist is unlikely to be interested in the rate of death of a dying star. He is going to be interested in social behavior of some kind.

More than likely he will be interested in only a limited area of human behavior. Because very few men can learn much about all human behavior, sociologists, like other scientists, specialize. Most sociologists are competent in more than one field, but few are competent in more than several fields. A sociologist may consider himself a social psychologist, an expert in minority group relations, and an urban sociologist. He may never work in industrial sociology or rural sociology or medical sociology. Specialization probably increases a sociologist's efficiency, but it also narrows his vision. Many motives help determine what kind of research interests a sociologist. Let us follow a sociologist who is a specialist in minority group relations as he goes about doing a piece of research to see how he works and why he picks a particular area to work in. The time is early in 1960.

Hopefully, our man (we shall call him Professor X) does not start his project with a blank mind. It is filled not only with the same kind of knowledge other people of his age and experience have, but also with sociological theories[1] about minority groups. Among other things he would have the following information in his mind:

1. A *minority group* is a group of people who are aware of themselves as a group and who meet some discrimination from other groups in the society. In the United States minority groups include Jews, Negroes, Indians, Orientals, Catholics, and others.

2. All groups, including minority groups, have *morale*. That is, their members have common values and are able to work together to achieve group goals.

3. Sometimes group morale is high, sometimes low. Both high and low morale are reflected in the behavior of group members.

4. Minority groups with high morale support their own members when possible.

This information lies dormant in Professor X's mind until one day when he gets into a discussion with a colleague on whether Republican Catholics are going to support John F. Kennedy, a Democrat, in the 1960 election because he is a Catholic.

Professor X sees the upcoming election as an opportunity to do some research. His motives are many and complex:

1. The study of group morale has been very fashionable lately and some of the research has stimulated Professor X to formulate some ideas of his own. He is aware that a study of group morale would be easily publishable, although this is probably not a major motive.

2. Professor X is professionally almost as much interested in political behavior as he is in minority groups. He has already formulated his ideas about group morale in political terms. He has undoubtedly taken into consideration the fact that this research will be simplified procedurally and financially if he can set up his study so that election returns can be used.

3. Some of Professor X's values add weight to his interest in doing the study. He is disturbed that the religious issue has been injected into the campaign and is unhappy that there is a possibility of bloc voting.

---

[1] Theories are nothing but systematic and detailed explanations of some portion of reality. In Chapter 2 we discussed the theory of the division of labor, for example. Theories, by the way, are very easy to think up. Proving them is the difficult thing.

Acting upon all these motives, Professor X decides to study Catholic voting in the 1960 election. He will, of course, need some money to do the study, and he decides to ask for it from a foundation that has funds available for research. The foundation will naturally want to know what this study will add to scientific knowledge before it gives away money, so Professor X writes out a proposal in which he explains the purpose of his research.

Professor X has decided that if Republican Catholics vote for Kennedy in large numbers, this would be an example of the effects of high group morale in a religious minority group. He writes down everything he knows about group morale which has been discovered by past studies and which is generally accepted by other sociologists as an explanation (theory) of group morale. This includes, among other things, what morale is, what kinds of situations produce high morale, how high group morale affects the behavior of individual group members, and so on. He ends this part of his proposal with a hypothesis.[2]

A hypothesis is a tentative prediction. The first part of the hypothesis starts with the word *if* and says *if this theory is true*; the second part starts with *then* and says *then we can expect to find this kind of behavior*. Professor X's hypothesis might read: If a minority group has high morale, then its members will support a member under attack.

His next step is to translate his hypothesis into something he can study. A translation of his hypothesis might read: Catholics are a minority group with high morale and will, therefore, vote for Kennedy in greater proportion than they did for previous Democratic Presidential candidates because Kennedy is under attack for his Catholicism.

Professor X still has to explain how he is going to do his research. One of the first problems is to locate a group of Catholics to study. Religious affiliation is not asked by the U.S. *Census,* so he cannot look there. He might look in a city telephone directory to find the location of Catholic churches. Most Catholic churches are neighborhood churches, so that one could assume that wherever there is a Catholic church there are Catholics living in the area. One could not assume, however, that most people in the neighborhood are Catholic. Civic leaders or heads of public agencies would probably be able to tell Professor X the areas of a city in which many people of Mexican, Italian, Irish, or Polish

---

[2] This is a simplification. If Professor X really expected to get any money, he would have to present half a dozen hypotheses. They would be in the same form as the one we are presenting.

descent live. Most of them are likely to be Catholic, and they frequently (but not always) live in separate neighborhoods.

Professor X, however, would not want to study these big-city groups, because they usually vote Democratic. If they were to vote for Kennedy, it could not be assumed that they had done so because both he and they were Catholic. Rather Professor X would look for an area in which most of the inhabitants are Catholic and habitually vote Republican. He could then study changes in their voting behavior from 1952 and 1956, when there was no Catholic Presidential candidate, to 1960 when there was. He would try to find a rural, Catholic, Republican county. Again, he would have to look for traditionally Catholic nationality groups who have settled in rural areas.

He would also like to find more than one area to study since local conditions might affect voting behavior in a single area. Voters might, for example, shift to the Democratic ticket in reaction to a poor, local Republican administration or to a local problem such as high unemployment, rather than because they identify with Kennedy as a Catholic.

Professor X also has to offer some way of proving that the Catholics he studies have high morale. He may have available descriptions of the past history of the counties which indicate this, or he may decide to do a questionnaire survey of community leaders and/or a sample of the residents, or he may use both techniques. This also goes into the proposal.

Professor X gets his money. He builds a questionnaire designed to find out if the Catholics being studied exhibit high group morale. He administers the questionnaire and interprets the findings. They show high group morale among the Catholics. Notice that Professor X has done most of his work on the basis of past knowledge before he has made any field observations at all. After the election he hires a graduate student to compare the votes for Kennedy with the number of votes for the Democratic presidential candidates in 1952 and 1956 in the counties he is studying. He adjusts for population changes and local conditions, tests to see if the difference is significant,[3] and comes to the conclusion that Catholics *did* vote more heavily for the Catholic, Democratic, Presidential candidate in 1960 then they had in 1952 and 1956. He feels justified in concluding that this does indicate that a minority group with high group morale will demonstrate it by supporting one of their members under attack for belonging to the minority group. Sociological theories about bloc voting as an indication of high minority group

---

[3] This is a technical term which indicates that the results of a statistical analysis have not occurred by chance alone.

morale have been strengthened. They cannot be proved, however, with one study. Before they can be regarded as proved, they must be tested by a large number of similar cases of minority group behavior. At some point sociologists can use this theory to predict behavior. They can say with assurance how minority groups would vote under specified circumstances. *The ability to predict accurately is the aim of all science.* It should be noted that if Professor X had found that Catholics did not vote heavily for Kennedy, this would have been just as important to science because it would have shown the theory to be wrong in some respect.

Research Techniques

The research techniques sociologists use may be no more complicated than those Professor X used. When necessary, however, difficult and complicated mathematical and statistical techniques may be employed. The researcher may gather his data by questionnaire or interview. Questionnaires can be designed to get at unconscious attitudes and motives. They are called *projective tests* because they are constructed in such a way that unconscious elements are projected into the responses. Interviews may be short and guided by a questionnaire, or they may be long and probing— *depth interviews.*

Sociologists sometimes do *content analysis.* That is, they count the number of times words or ideas or stereotypes or attitudes appear in a given context. This technique is used to analyze the mass media (newspapers, TV and radio programs, magazines). It may also be used to analyze fiction, poetry, or even public-school textbooks. Content studies which showed that certain minority groups were inevitably depicted as menials, villains, or fools have done much to change stories in magazines with national circulation. The material in TV advertising and programming has also been altered to give a more realistic portrayal of minorities. It should be added that the studies alone did not produce changes. Militant minorities used the studies to buttress their protests.

An important method in sociology is *historical analysis.* The sociologist goes to the historian for evidence to support his theory. Comparative studies of large groups like city neighborhoods or unions or nations are likely to be based on historical materials. One sociologist studied the history of land values over 100 years in Chicago. Some have studied patterns of migration, and others have compared the development of cities in Europe and America.[4] Whenever an individual or event is representative in most respects of a

---

[4] For other examples of historical analysis, see pp. 2–3 and pp. 15–16.

category of individuals or events, sociologists can make a careful and detailed study of a single case and reasonably generalize from that case to the whole category. Intensive research of this kind is called a *case study.* The detailed history of a garment workers' union local can tell us much about other locals in the same union. Case studies make it easier to compare phenomena, as, for example, a typical garment workers' local with a typical boilermakers' local. Case studies are useful in tracing changes over time; e.g., the stages a business passes through as it moves from one-man ownership to a corporation structure.

One kind of case study is the *life history*—a chronological account of the important events in an individual's life which reveals the experiences and events that have most influenced his behavior. A famous life history—*The Jack Roller* (1930)—recounts the life history of a criminal, through which sociologists hoped to better understand the motives that lead to a criminal career.

Sometimes sociologists take groups into laboratories and conduct *experiments* under controlled conditions. They may try to create group solidarity and high morale in the groups under study and then see if they can be broken down and by what methods. One is never sure, however, that the groups in the laboratory are representative of social groups outside the laboratory. Whenever possible, sociologists prefer to study social groups outside the laboratory—boy scout troops, hospital wards, a union local, a department in a factory, a public-school class. The sociologist who was refused permission to study real juries asked citizens on the official jury lists to serve on mock juries. Once a mock jury was assembled, he presented real cases to them in exactly the same manner as the original cases had been tried in court. Their deliberations were recorded, then studied to see how the mock juries arrived at their decisions. This is not as satisfactory as a study of a real jury. The mock juries, made up of a cross section of citizens, were, however, more like real juries than the usual laboratory groups composed of college students could possibly be.

Sometimes a sociologist will keep careful records of what goes on in a group of which he is a member so that he may study it. Because a sociologist shares the aims and values of any group he belongs to, he may not be objective in his analysis. On the other hand, he has access to the feelings of members of the group out-siders might have difficulty in perceiving. Some groups, like religious sects or criminal gangs, are difficult to study because their activities are secret. At times researchers have pretended to be members of a closed group to find out what went on in the group. Sociologists, for example, have entered prisons and pretended to be criminals.

One member of a team of social psychologists joined a sect that believed in the imminent end of the world and stayed in the group until the appointed day had come and gone in order to find out how the group would react when their beliefs were not fulfilled. This technique of studying groups is called *participant observation.*

One research method peculiar to sociology is the *ideal-type method,* invented by Max Weber. It is a technique for *comparing complex social phenomena.* The technique requires the researcher to construct models of whatever phenomena are being compared. These are perhaps similar to the miniature models a city planner prepares when he is trying to show his client how a reconstructed area of the city will look. All the pieces are in proper proportion and stand in the same place as the completed buildings will stand; but the buildings have no windows or interiors, trees and grass are represented by green paint, and so on. Ideal types, although they are verbal rather than three dimensional, are like the planner's models in that they include only the broad outlines that define the phenomena and neglect the details.

For example, Robert Merton has constructed four ideal types of people in regard to their attitudes toward discrimination and their prejudice against minorities. They are:

1. the unprejudiced nondiscriminator, or all-weather liberal
2. the unprejudiced discriminator, or fair-weather liberal
3. the prejudiced nondiscriminator, or fair-weather illiberal
4. the prejudiced discriminator, or all-weather illiberal

Merton's types are not logical categories but descriptions built out of careful and repeated observations. Only those traits that are always present and causally important are included.

Sociologists use these and many other techniques when they do research, and they may use several procedures in a single study. Anything that works is acceptable, and new methods of research are constantly being discovered and tried out. How to use research techniques, what constitutes good procedure, and under what circumstances one or another method is suitable are learned as a part of professional training. The layman, reading a piece of research, cannot usually judge the value of the techniques. He can, however, observe whether all the steps Professor X went through have been carried out. Frequently, important steps in research procedure are omitted, and the results of the research are then of doubtful value.

Not All Research Is Valuable

Let us examine the work of another sociologist. Professor Y, also an expert in minority group relations, is interested in seeing whether a film to which he has access will reduce prejudice in school children. He secures permission to show the movie to all the fifth-grade children in the public schools of a Midwestern city we shall call Centertown. Before he shows the film, he tests the children to see how much and what kind of prejudice they have against Negro children. It is assumed that tests can indicate prejudice or lack of it and that Professor Y administers them properly. Then he shows the film to one-half of the classes, chosen at random. Afterwards, he tests all the children again for indications of prejudice against Negro children. He finds there has been a significant reduction of prejudice among the children who saw the movie, and only among those children.[5] He concludes that the movie does reduce the expression of race prejudice, at least immediately after the subjects have seen the film. Professor Y's techniques are impeccable, and there is little doubt that he has done what he claims to have done. He has reduced prejudice among those fifth-grade children in Centertown who saw the film; but, because he did not specify any theory as to what causes prejudice or relate the content of the movie to the theory by using an hypothesis, we have no idea of *why* the children lost their prejudice. We would have no indication of whether the movie would work equally well on another group. We cannot generalize. We can make no predictions on the basis of this study.

Imagine that Professor Y had started with one of the generally accepted theories of prejudice: Most white people have little contact with Negroes. They see them only in menial jobs or through derogatory stereotypes in fiction or the mass media. When whites can see Negroes in situations like their own, their prejudice may be reduced. Imagine also that the movie shows middle-class Negro children engaging in the kind of activities usual with middle-class, Midwestern white children. When Midwestern white children who have little direct contact with Negroes see a movie showing Negro children to be much like themselves, then the prejudice of the white children will be reduced. If Professor Y had stated his theory and hypothesis, then the basic theory—that *equal-status contacts* reduce prejudice—would have been strengthened. We would also know that if we want to try to reduce prejudice in the future we should try to increase equal-status contacts, whether by a movie or some other method. Unfortunately, there are far more Professor Y's than

---

[5] The classes which do not see the movie are the *control group*. If the children in these classes had lost some of their prejudice between the first and second times they were tested, the researcher would conclude that something other than the movie had been operating to reduce prejudice.

Professor X's, and research not firmly anchored in theory is very common, even in professional journals.

THEORIES MUST BEGIN SOMEWHERE

So far we have been dealing with research in fields where there is an established body of sociological theory to be refined and made more precise. How does a sociologist proceed when he is a pioneer in the field? He uses his common sense and hopes that he will lay a foundation on which later research can build. In 1928 Emory S. Bogardus published a *social distance scale*. He had asked nearly 2,000 Americans about their attitudes toward forty racial, nationality, and religious groups in the following situations:

1. would admit to close kinship by marriage
2. would admit to a club as personal friends
3. would admit to residence on the same street as neighbors
4. would admit to employment in the same firm or factory
5. would admit to citizenship in the United States
6. would admit as visitors to the United States
7. would exclude from the country

Most of the respondents were willing to admit British, native white Americans, and Canadians to the close intimacy of marriage. The social distance they wished to keep between themselves and these three groups was small. On the other hand, the social distance they wished to keep between themselves and Negroes, Japanese, Jews, Chinese, Hindus, and Turks was large. Sometimes they did not even want them to enter the country. Other groups, like the French, Spaniards, and Italians, were kept at an intermediate social distance.

Bogardus had no theory except the common-sense observation that some groups in the United States were more discriminated against than others. His social scale was so ingenious and useful a measure of discrimination, however, that many students of discrimination began using it and developing variations of it. Sociologists were surprised to find that Negroes, Jews, Chinese, and Japanese also wished to keep the same social distance between themselves and other groups, except that Negroes accepted Negroes, Jews preferred Jews, and so on. Sociologists had hypothesized that minority groups would show less prejudice. They then developed the theory that prejudice is part of American culture and that minority groups learn it just as the majority group does. This gradual accumulation of research around a narrow subject, each study reinforcing and refining the theory, is the way basic theory is built.[6]

One of the results of wishing to keep social distance between one's self and others is discrimination. In the United States discrimination is much sharper in some areas than in others. Gunnar Myrdal, in *An American Dilemma*,[7] postulated a *rank order of discrimination*. The white man's rank order of discrimination is as follows:

Rank 1.   The bar against intermarriage and sexual intercourse involving white women.

Rank 2.   The discrimination against equality in social relations, such as dancing, swimming, eating, or drinking together.

Rank 3.   Discrimination in the use of public facilities, such as schools and churches.

Rank 4.   Political disfranchisement.

Rank 5.   Discrimination in law courts, by the police, and by other public servants.

Rank 6.   Discrimination in economic activities and in access to public relief and other welfare facilities.

According to Myrdal's theory, the higher in rank the behavior, the more resistant the white population will be to granting equality in that field. Myrdal also stated that the Negro's own rank order is in inverse relation to that of the white man. The higher rank the discrimination, the less interested he is in breaking it down. By and large, Negroes concentrated their first efforts against discrimination in the ranks of least sensitivity, as Myrdal advised they should. The high resistance to school desegregation, in both North and South, as compared to the relatively low resistance to integrating Negroes into factory work shows how accurate this theory is.

It is hoped that from this chapter the reader will have acquired some idea of how a sociologist goes about his work. The chapter also illustrates the way in which sociological theory is refined bit by bit, each researcher adding his small share, until a theory is either proved or discarded as useless. The next chapter will describe some of the research which has been useful in building sociological theory.

---

[6] A summary of the research done with Bogardus' social distance scale and variations of it can be found in George E. Simpson and J. Milton Yinger, *Racial and Cultural Minorities* (New York: Harper & Row, Publishers, 1965), pp. 112–17.

[7] With the assistance of Richard Sterner and Arnold M. Rose (New York: Harper & Row, Publishers, 1st ed. 1944), pp. 60–67 of 1962 ed.

Significant Research in Sociology: Past and Present

chapter four

THE FIRST EMPIRICAL RESEARCH

In France in 1897, Emile Durkheim published a book called *Suicide*, the first piece of empirical sociological research. There had been careful compilations of fact before this and much theorizing without empirical support. In *Suicide* for the first time a major sociological theory was tested with carefully collected statistical data.

Durkheim could not find consistent associations between suicide and such factors as age, nationality, marital status, rural-urban residence, and education. He did find suicide associated with certain kinds of relationships between the individual and his society. He concluded that suicides could be classified and explained in three ways:

1. *Altruistic suicide:* The sacrifice of one's life for others, as when a soldier, for the good of his platoon, undertakes a mission from which he knows he will not escape. In this kind of suicide the individual identifies himself so closely with other members of the group that the survival of the group becomes for him the same as his own survival.
2. *Egoistic suicide:* Suicide committed by individuals who are detached from the group—the mentally ill, for example.
3. *Anomic suicide:* Suicide resulting from sudden disorganization of a society because of large-scale catastrophes or rapid social change.

The concept *anomie*, derived from the study of anomic suicide, has become one of the basic concepts of sociology because it describes the breaking of the bond which holds individuals to their groups. Durkheim's study was the first empirical demonstration of the fact that an individual cannot survive apart from a group and of some of the complicated relationships between an individual and the society to which he belongs.

The first major piece of empirical research accomplished in the United States was *The Polish Peasant in Europe and America* by William I. Thomas and Florian Znaniecki, published in 1919–21. At this period in American history, there was considerable study of the problems of immigrants, but it was limited largely to their economic and housing conditions. Thomas and Znaniecki were interested in how people raised in small, cohesive, rural villages adjusted their behavior when transplanted to large cities in an industrialized society. They followed the life stories of a number of immigrants from Poland by analyzing the contents of letters sent between the immigrants and their friends and relatives in Poland. They demonstrated that an individual tries to maintain a consistent pattern of social behavior, even when the social situation in which he lives changes drastically. The results, of course, are often mental illness, disorganization, and criminal behavior, because his internalized expectations of the society are unrealistic.

THE CHICAGO SOCIOLOGISTS STUDY THEIR CITY

At the University of Chicago, under the influence of Robert E. Park (1864–1944), sociologists in the 1920's and the 1930's began to do research on urban problems. After World War I, Chicago was a fast growing city, spreading over the surrounding, seemingly endless prairies. New neighborhoods sprang up. The inhabitants were divided into many racial and nationality groups, some of them newly arrived from Europe, some of them migrants from America's rural areas. Change was rapid; heterogeneity great; the political structure inadequate to deal with either. The Chicago sociologists, stimulated by Park's sensitivity to urban life (he had started his career as a journalist), saw the city as a great social laboratory spread before them, and as such they used it.

The Chicago studies—there were nineteen of them published between 1923 and 1933—are colorful and interesting. Louis Wirth's *The Ghetto* (1925) is a study of the effects of social isolation on a minority group. It is still a standard work. The first intimate study of a juvenile gang was Frederick Thrasher's *The Gang* (1927). No better study on the subject has yet been done. The heterogeneity of a big city was analyzed in Harvey Zorbaugh's *The Gold Coast and the Slum* (1929). The first attempts to map the geographic incidence of social problems was done in a book called *Delinquency Areas* (1929).[1] Taken together the Chicago studies form a solid theoretical and empirical foundation for urban sociology, and they are still important.

SOCIOLOGISTS REFINE THEIR PREDICTIVE TECHNIQUES

If prediction is the aim of science, it is not surprising that prediction studies have been a major concern of sociologists. When the Social Science Research Council published a comprehensive evaluation of prediction studies in 1941,[2] a study by E. W. Burgess and Leonard S. Cottrell, *Predicting Success or Failure in Marriage* (1939), was rated highly for its ability to predict accurately. Burgess and Cottrell used a questionnaire to discover the degree of happiness of their subjects and then tested the respondent's answers for accuracy and truthfulness in a variety of ways. They were then able to pick out those items on the questionnaire which predicted either success or failure in achieving happiness in marriage. The items which predicted well became the basis for a standardized test. Length of courtship, age at marriage, happiness of parents, degree of participation in church and other group activities, and attitudes toward sex were some of the factors predictive of marital happiness. It should be emphasized, however, that single items from the test do not have predictive value.

It is hard to overemphasize the importance of this pioneering study. The development of highly predictive tests has had much practical value. Marital adjustment tests are used by marriage counselors, social workers, ministers, and others as a basis for advising their clients and as an aid in diagnosing the cause of marital difficulties. The predictive technique Burgess and Cottrell invented has been refined and applied to other fields. A test was developed for the army in World War II to screen out potential psychoneurotics. There are tests which predict success or failure on parole. Others indicate potential success in certain jobs.

---

[1] Clifford Shaw *et al.*

[2] Paul Horst (ed.), *The Prediction of Personal Adjustment* (New York: The Social Science Research Council, 1941).

Delinquent or psychoneurotic behavior among children can also be predicted.

SOCIAL CHANGE AND PREDICTION

If one understands why social change occurs, one should be able to predict its results. Sociologists during the 1930's studied social trends for exactly this reason. Because they concentrated their attention mainly on economic factors, social trend research failed to predict accurately when other factors were important. It was impossible also to take into account the effects of major and unanticipated social events like World War II. Demographers, for example, usually assume that birth and death rates will vary to some extent, but they were unable to predict either the great baby boom of war and postwar days or the lowering of the death rate among the elderly due to new medical discoveries. As a consequence, all the population projections made before 1940 were much too low.

Several modern social trend studies have, however, been able to predict accurately, mainly because they took a large number of factors into account. One of these is Arnold Rose's *The Negro's Morale* (1949). Starting with slavery days, he analyzed the factors which created solidarity among the Negroes: increased literacy; the work of the Negro press in maintaining communication throughout the Negro community; devoted and effective leadership organized into protest organizations with specific and realizable aims; the success of the segregated Negro church in producing an in-group feeling; heavy migration of Negroes to the North; changes in the economic and social structure of the South, and changes in the attitudes of the white population, both North and South. He noted the ways in which increasing in-group feeling enabled the Negroes to mount an effective protest against discrimination. In 1949 he predicted approximately when and how the Negro protest would break out. The sit-ins, boycotts, and riots with which Negroes have attempted to gain their civil rights, starting in 1961, generally fulfilled his predictions.

The method of predicting used in *The Negro's Morale* was formulated by Gunnar Myrdal in *An American Dilemma* (1944). Myrdal is an economist, and his technique for predicting social changes is borrowed from economics. He calls his theoretical model the *principle of cumulative causation*. He assumes that all the factors relevant to any social change are connected in a spiral, which is moving either up or down. Any change in any of the factors will affect all the other factors and move them in the same direction as the original change was moving. For example, an increase in the educational attainments of Negroes will increase their ability to get well-paying jobs which in turn will enable them to buy better housing. Conversely, an increase in unemployment will decrease their ability to buy better housing and, because better schools are in good neighborhoods, will also decrease the possibility of getting an adequate education. This model for analyzing social change can also serve as a guide to governmental action. If Negroes are suffering from greater than average unemployment because of discrimination or low educational attainments or both, a law to prevent job discrimination and policies to increase educational opportunities will decrease unemployment. This will start the spiral of connected factors moving upwards, and it will continue under its own momentum.

COMMUNITY STUDIES

Although a society does not have to have a geographic base to be a society, some societies, like the United States, do have one. When they do, they are called *communities*. Sociological interest in studying communities goes back at least as far as the publication of W. E. B. Du Bois' study *The Philadelphia Negro* in 1899. In 1929 Robert and Helen Lynd made sociological history by publishing their famous study of Muncie, Indiana, called *Middletown*. The Lynds were trying to study the community as a whole. They went to live in Muncie and interviewed the people they met and lived with, in the same manner as anthropologists live with and interview the groups they study.

The Lynds found the Middletown economy dominated by one industry. The class structure of the community was rigid, and there was a lack of communication among groups. Participation in community affairs was confined to a few people. Middletown citizens were portrayed as unhappy and sullen.[3] Eight years later, a second volume, *Middletown in Transition*, examined the social changes the Great Depression had caused in Muncie. Economic

---

[3] The citizens of Middletown were quite unhappy when the Lynds exposed the details of their community life to a national audience. John Marquand took a more lighthearted view of the observing sociologist in his satiric and very funny novel, *Point of No Return*, about the invasion of a New England town by a group of sociologists intent on studying the inhabitants. There are no reports on how the sociologists felt about being analyzed by Marquand.

and political power was more dispersed throughout the community; there was great participation of all groups; and the citizens were much more aware of and affected by trends in the national economy.

Somewhat later (1941), W. Lloyd Warner and his associates, also using anthropological techniques, studied a New England town they called Yankee City. The results of this study were published in five volumes, each on a specialized subject. Taken together they describe the entire community. The Yankee City studies aroused controversy about the class structure of American society, which has not simmered down yet. Warner said that Yankee City residents regarded themselves and others as belonging to six different classes: lower-lower; upper-lower; lower-middle; upper-middle; lower-upper; and upper-upper. He implied that the total American class structure was similarly divided. Critics of Warner say that his classification cannot be applied in large metropolitan areas or the nation as a whole, because people do not know each other well enough to make a judgment about the class everybody belongs to. The critics seek objective criteria of class, like income or occupation. As a rule, sociologists today avoid the problem. They study differences in occupation, income, education, prestige, and status, but avoid defining classes as such.

Equally controversial was Warner's declaration (made before the publication of the Yankee City books) that Negroes constituted a caste in American society. It shocked Americans to think that other Americans were relegated to a separate category from which they were prevented from moving by law and custom. John Dollard, in his book *Caste and Class in a Southern Town* (1937), studied the extent to which segregation created a society in which people's occupations, behavior, and attitudes were fixed by their caste positions. Dollard's findings supported Warner's caste theory as did Hylan Lewis' study of the Negro section of a Southern town (*Blackways of Kent,* 1955). St. Clair Drake and Horace Cayton studied a Northern Negro community (in Chicago) and found such extreme discrimination there that the community was unable to function (*Black Metropolis,* 1945).

Both the Middletown studies and the Yankee City series were landmarks in sociology, but in dealing with the community as a whole they failed to do justice to the complexity of a modern city. They also neglected the ways in which even small towns are affected by national political policies or the condition of the national economy. James West published a study of a small, isolated Missouri town (*Plainville, U.S.A.*) in 1946. When Art Gallaher, Jr., studied the same town (*Plainville, Fifteen Years Later,* 1961), he found that economic changes in the United States had completely destroyed the isolation of the town and had changed most of the attitudes West had regarded as characteristic of the residents.

In the interest of greater completeness, later community studies have concentrated on only one aspect of a community. In *Elmtown's Youth* (1949), for example, A. B. Hollingshead studied only the youth of his community. He found that economic and social differences among the young people set them apart in their interests and aspirations, even in early adolescence.

Because large numbers of Americans now live in suburbs, studies of suburban life have been of recent interest. William M. Dobriner, in *The Suburban Community* (1958), puts to rest some of the stereotypes about suburban life. There are many kinds of suburbs inhabited by people who shortly before lived in cities. Suburban life is, therefore, not all of a piece, nor does it differ much from city life. Robert C. Wood (*Suburbia, Its People and Their Politics*, 1963) supports Dobriner's findings by examining the ways in which people express their needs and interests through a variety of political activities.

In view of this long sociological interest in community studies, it is somewhat disconcerting for a sociologist to realize that one of the best community studies of recent years has been done by a political scientist.[4] It does point up how the social sciences overlap in their interests, their conceptual schemes, and their methodology. Robert A. Dahl's book *Who Governs? Democracy and Power in an American City* (1961), a beautifully executed and highly informative piece of research, illustrates the more recent, segmentalized approach to the study of the community. Dahl is interested in only one aspect of community life—its politics—and in only one aspect of politics—who has power in a middle-sized New England city (New Haven, Connecticut) and how it is acquired and used.[5] He feels that political *power* (the ability to impose one's will on others) is widely dispersed in American communities and differentially used.

By analyzing the political history of New Haven from colonial days until 1960, Dahl is able to show that political power has shifted from the hands of an elite social group to those of professional politicians, representative of and responsive to the demands

---

[4] History repeats itself. The very earliest community studies in the United States were made by a group of political scientists at Johns Hopkins University in the 1880's.

[5] It is hoped that those who believe politics is a mystery beyond the control of the average citizen will read Dahl's fine book.

of the average citizen. In addition, he uses case studies to illustrate how and when the average citizen exerts his normally latent political power.

Dahl's theories about political behavior are in contrast to those expressed by C. Wright Mills, a sociologist, in a well-known book *The Power Elite* (1956). Mills believed that the well-to-do were also the economically and politically powerful. His work has been criticized because he did not demonstrate that having great wealth is the same as exerting great economic power. Economic power belongs to the managers of industry, but in the United States they are not the same group as the wealthy, although these groups may overlap. The owners and managers of industry are often in competition with each other, and they may have regional interests. Moreover, Mills did not demonstrate that the economically powerful controlled the political system. The President of the United States has enormous political power, but he may be a man of modest means, like Truman; a career officer, like Eisenhower; or an heir to great wealth with comparatively little economic power, like Kennedy. Members of Congress exhibit the same range of economic and social status.

Floyd Hunter, in his study of Atlanta, Georgia, *Community Power Structure* (1953), agrees to some extent with Mills. He stated that a small, economically and socially powerful group exerted great political influence in the local community.

Dahl's research was undertaken, in part, to disprove the Hunter-Mills thesis. His findings, buttressed by impressive empirical and documentary evidence, do call both Hunter's and Mills' theories into question. Whether Dahl's analysis can be applied to a large Southern city like Atlanta or to the United States as a whole is a question that waits upon further research.

DEVIANT BEHAVIOR

Sociologists have done many studies on deviant behavior— alcoholism, narcotic addiction, gambling, illegitimacy, prostitution, adult crime, and juvenile delinquency. Deviant behavior is one type of social problem. The term "deviant" assumes that most people in the society disapprove of and do not engage in this kind of behavior. If this were true, it would simplify life for sociologists. Although most people will verbally disapprove of what is classified as deviant behavior, most people engage in some kinds of deviant behavior some of the time. Disapproval really falls on those who get caught. Furthermore, all groups in a society are not agreed on what deviant behavior is. For sociologists studying deviant behavior, there is another set of tension-producing circumstances: What they recommend to cure deviant behavior, on the basis of the very best scientific evidence they can muster, is frequently unacceptable to the society. This makes sociologists very vulnerable to the suggestion that they should stop studying deviant behavior and instead find out how to get a society to change its values.

For example, those groups in the United States who habitually consume alcohol during meals and give their children liquor at an early age are the groups which do *not* produce alcoholics. Research seems to show that the habitual but restrained use of alcohol is a safeguard against alcoholism.[6] The United States is the only modern country with a high rate of drug addiction. Other countries give addicts what drugs they need under medical supervision, thus taking the profit out of the illicit drug trade and preventing addicts from engaging in crime to get the money they need to pay for drugs. Americans are unwilling to follow the advice of sociologists in either of these two situations.

Edwin H. Sutherland is responsible for two significant pieces of research in criminology. They are significant because they introduced new ideas and stimulated a great deal of subsequent research along the same lines. The first was *The Professional Thief* (1937), which pointed out that the most successful criminals were professionals, who entered into and learned their occupations in exactly the way a doctor, judge, or carpenter learns his. *White-Collar Crime* (1949) documented the fact that many crimes, costly to the society, were committed by otherwise respectable citizens and corporations. These two studies established the idea that ordinary people engage in deviant behavior. If society offers the opportunity, people learn deviant behavior in the same way they learn acceptable ways of behaving.

Recent studies of juvenile delinquency have sought to find out what it is either in the society or in the training of children that makes them susceptible to learning deviant behavior. An excellent study of this kind is Clark Vincent's *Unmarried Mothers* (1961). No single set of circumstances is responsible for illicit sexual activities, but Vincent does succeed in isolating some of

---

[6] For a comprehensive survey of research on alcoholism, see David J. Pittman and Charles R. Snyder, *Society, Culture and Drinking Patterns* (New York: John Wiley & Sons, Inc., 1962).

the factors which prevent young girls from internalizing traditional sex values.

A similar and very influential study is Albert Cohen's *Delinquent Boys, the Culture of the Gang* (1955). Gang behavior is frequently characteristic of lower-class males. They enter delinquent gangs in the same way and for the same reasons that middle-class boys enter Boy Scout troops. They evidently get the same kinds of personal satisfaction in the gang as other boys get from scout troops. The culture (meanings and values) of the gang is, however, mischievous and anti-social. The gang members are socialized into this deviant culture. If the culture of the family and school have been firmly internalized, socialization into the gang is prevented. Among lower classes, there is either inadequate family socialization or its culture is close to gang culture. There is a high correlation between gang membership and school failure. Since boys enter school many years before they typically enter a gang, we can conclude that the school has not been able to socialize these boys either.

Most of sociology consists of reports and analyses of research studies. What has been presented in this chapter is an arbitrary sampling of the most significant studies conducted by sociologists. It should be noted that good research is not necessarily recent research and that some of the earliest studies are as important today as when they were done. On the other hand some research—like Sutherland's or Myrdal's—introduces new ideas, starts research in new directions, and outmodes older work.

The next chapter will present the most significant findings of sociology. Sometimes it will be evident to the reader that the supporting research has been reported in this or earlier sections. If not, the reader should assume that there is research which documents or supports the statements.

The Fundamental Insights of Sociology
chapter five

At the end of the first chapter, the reader was introduced to the idea of the "sociological perspective"—the special point of view of sociologists. Each succeeding chapter has attempted to give definition and specificity to the sociological perspective.

The first part of Chapter 2 pointed out the importance of the cosmopolitanism of sociology, both in the past and today, for establishing the possibility of universal generalizations. The second part of Chapter 2 traced the growth of sophisticated theory, adequate to explain the complexity of social reality. In Chapter 3 we explored the ways sociologists have adapted scientific methodology to the study of social data and looked into some of the ingenious ways sociologists have solved their research problems. Chapter 4 examined many of the research accomplishments of sociology to display both the range of sociological interests and the conclusions yielded by studies.

Chapter 5 contains those insights (expressed sometimes as definitions and assumptions, other times as generalizations, concepts, or theories) sociologists regard as the core of their perspective. These insights, taken together, enable sociologists to put order into observed human behavior in such a fashion that they can understand how it is caused.

The term "perspective" is relevant in another way. Sociological theory has been constructed by viewing social data from a number of viewpoints. The concept of role, for example, has one dimension when viewed as individual behavior; another when seen as a constituent of culture; and a third when described as a part of social structure. The family can be viewed as the prototype of a primary group, as a socializing agency, or as an institution. In this chapter, then, society will be analyzed from a series of viewpoints, focusing successively on the individual, the group, culture, and social process, while at the same time keeping entirely within the specialized approach of sociology.

THE INDIVIDUAL AND THE GROUP

The individual and the group are the two poles about which sociological theory revolves. Everybody is born into an on-going group. This is likely to be a family. The group precedes the individual, and the social traits of the individual are inculcated by the group; the individual takes over and internalizes the meanings and values of the group and thus becomes both a member of the group and a socialized individual. The process by which this is accomplished is called socialization and occurs in the following manner:

SOCIALIZATION

In the family parents and siblings expect certain things of the young child. When the child does something the parents consider undesirable, they say, "No, no," and accompany these words with a frown or by nodding their head from side to side, or even by slapping the child's hands. The child thus learns what the parents expect (what they mean and what they value) when they use the words, "No, no," or any of the usual accompanying gestures.

At some point, the child can and does say to himself, "Johnny, no, no," and responds to the expectations he himself has raised by refraining from doing something he has learned to expect will bring negative reactions. The child has put himself into his parent's place. He has become an object to himself just as he has been an object to his parents. He begins to see himself as others see him, to evaluate his behavior and appearance as he thinks others are evaluating them, and to have a sense of shame or pride about the evaluations he thinks others make of him. He acquires an image of himself reflected by the attitudes of others just as if he saw himself in a looking-glass. His social self has emerged. He is beginning to be socialized. The social self is the end product of the process of socialization.

The social self emerges somewhere around the age of two. Until that time the expectations directed toward a child are those suitable to his age. But at two a child has been able to internalize only a small part of the society to which he belongs. He is not a full-fledged member of his own family. He will not yet have had contacts with his neighborhood or with the school which he will surely have later. As he learns what his family expects of him at later ages and what kinds of behavior his neighbors and his teachers and his peers expect, he will become more socialized. He internalizes a greater variety of expectations coming to him from more and different people. During the whole of life, whenever one enters a new group and internalizes the expectations of the other group members, socialization takes place.

Unsocialized individuals are not fully human. Babies kept in hospitals or orphanages for the first few months of their lives fail to develop either physically or mentally. When nurses are told to pick up the babies regularly and fondle and caress them as a mother does, the children begin to develop normally. At this age expectations consist of gestures and meaningless verbalizations, but some kind of communication, even though it is simple, is evidently essential for human development. Children whose parents direct contradictory expectations toward them, being severe today and permissive tomorrow, fail to become adequately socialized because they never can learn what is expected of them. Their self-image is distorted as if there were defects in the looking-glass in which they see themselves. Some mentally ill people can be described as inadequately socialized in this same way.

Individuals can also become desocialized. The Communist technique of brain-washing is a technique for desocialization. Although the precipitating causes of mental illness are manifold, many of the mentally ill can be described as desocialized.[1] Prisoners returning to society and those confined to hospitals for a long period must be resocialized to some extent. This is why criminologists and psychiatrists try to keep people out of institutions in the first place and recommend half-way houses for returnees in which resocialization into the larger society can take place.

Roles. Expectations, important components of socialization, can be further analyzed from the point of view of individual behavior. The expectations directed toward an individual during socialization are not random and unorganized. Group members have in their minds certain *sets of organized meanings and values called roles.* It is these roles they direct toward others, and it is roles, rather than separate expectations, that are internalized. Once a role is internalized an individual can direct his behavior in accordance with it. For example, "Wash your hands," "Sit up straight," "Don't hit your sister" are a few of the enormous number

---

[1] When the society is so disorganized that a large number of individuals become desocialized, *anomie* is said to be present. See pp. 33–34.

of expectations that make up the role of the "well-behaved middle-class boy." They imply certain values. Expectations can be conveyed positively—by approval and rewards—as well as negatively, and they are as often conveyed subtly as directly.

As a result of the constant flow of expectations of any group, the member has a general idea of how he is expected to behave. He knows what his roles are. The role of mother in American suburban culture includes preparing meals for her children, taking them to the dentist, reading to them, supervising their TV programs, and belonging to the PTA. In some cultures the role of mother includes very little more than bearing children and taking minimal care of them for two or three years. Strictly speaking, a role does not refer to acted-out behavior but to ideas in the mind. It is better to think of roles in this way because, when the individual acts, his actions reflect a number of roles in his mind which he has integrated[2] in some way.

One does not act out pure roles. For example, when a mother gets up at two in the morning to give her baby a bottle, she may be acting out both the general role of "mother" and the more specific role of "responsible mother." She may also be manifesting the idea that the two o'clock feeding is part of the wife's job, her role, rather than that of the husband's. While the baby is nursing, the mother may be reading a book in preparation for a sociology examination the following week in pursuance of her role as student, or career woman, or that of the "wife who keeps up her intellectual interests."

Roles sometimes conflict. The contents of the role of mother and that of career woman may conflict, but if the individual is to act at all she must make some integration of the ideas that comprise these two roles. An action may reflect part of each role, or one role may not be acted out at any one moment. If one acts out one of a conflicting pair of roles at one point in time and the other role at some other time, one's actions become inconsistent. Studies have been made of the *role conflict* a child undergoes when the demands of home and school are not the same as those of his peer group. A worker who becomes a foreman can be torn between his loyalty to the company and his identification with the workers.

Primary Groups

A different kind of analysis can emerge when attention is shifted from the individual to the group. Sociologists are not only interested in what goes on *inside* the family. They also ask whether the family is a group specialized for accomplishing socialization

---

[2] It is the *I*, of course, that does the integrating. See p. 19.

and whether similar groups exist. They find that groups can be *differentiated by their structure*. By the structure of a group, sociologists mean the usual and typical kinds of relationships that take place among group members. The family is a *primary group* because it is the first group human beings participate in and because it is the group in which people learn the primary skills of interaction and communication (socialization). Some local neighborhoods, friendship groups, and some work groups also have the structure of a primary group. In small tribes or in small villages, the whole society may be one big primary group, although this was much more common in the past than today.

Common sense tells us that membership in a primary group is important to small children, but sociologists find that it is also important for adults. The importance of primary-group relationships to adults was discovered accidentally. Because there were too few psychiatrists in mental institutions to give all the patients the attention they needed, psychiatrists began to treat patients in groups. The improvement in the patients was little short of miraculous, and the doctors began to ask why. Inadvertently, they had established primary groups, and the patients were communicating and interacting with each other. Primary-group therapy is now well understood and has been extended from mental institutions to general hospitals to aid in faster recovery of patients. In advanced prisons, group therapy is used to rehabilitate prisoners. The success of Alcoholics Anonymous seems to depend on the primary-group contacts achieved within it. The Black Muslim movement, a small and aggressive Negro protest group, has had remarkable success in curing drug addiction among its members. This, too, seems to be the result of primary-group relationships.

The usefulness of establishing primary groups to handle social problems has led to new theoretical explanations of deviant groups. Chief among these are the explanations of delinquent gangs as primary groups in which children are socialized when the home or school has failed in socialization.[3]

Secondary Groups

Any group not a primary group is called a *secondary group*. Participation in secondary groups is impersonal, segmental (one does not express all his personality), and can be of short duration. Typically, one belongs to many secondary groups in

---

[3] An excellent summary of primary-group research centering around children's problems is contained in the first few chapters of Arno Jewett, Joseph Merand, and Doris V. Gunerson (eds.), *Improving English Skills of Culturally Different Youth in Large Cities* (Washington, D.C.: U.S. Department of Health, Education, and Welfare, 1964).

a modern, pluralistic society. All secondary groups are not structured alike. A widespread kind of secondary group in our society is the *bureaucracy*.

A bureaucracy is a hierarchical form of social organization, best represented by the diagram of a triangle with a few people at the top and many below. A bureaucracy is an orderly or rational kind of organization based on written rules. It is assumed that the few people at the top have most of the power, but also that they have it because they meet reasonable and specified requirements. The ways in which one moves from the bottom of the pyramid to the top are also clearly specified, as are the relationships among all the members of a bureaucracy. Bureaucracies are slow to change and have no mechanism for adaptation to individual needs. If it is not written down in the rules, it does not exist. The army is a good example of a bureaucracy. So are American governments, with their written constitutions. Industry, schools, unions, even large religious denominations, are organized hierarchically.

Another common kind of secondary group is the *voluntary association*. When people have some common interest or common problem, they frequently band together to pursue their interests or to solve the problem. The National Bridge Association, The American Medical Association, The Audubon Society, the Red Cross, the Boy Scouts, sororities and fraternities, political clubs, businessmen's and taxpayers' associations, unions, and farm organizations are examples of voluntary associations.

Voluntary associations try to keep their members informed on what is going on within their area of interest. When the members think legislation should be passed, they frequently act as pressure groups, as the National Education Association does, for example, on matters of education. Because voluntary associations are widespread over the country, their information-spreading and lobbying activities distribute political power and enable the individual citizen to exert a measure of direct control over his affairs.

The Relationships Between Primary and Secondary Groups

Some people show great ability to understand bureaucratic structures and can fulfill their needs and rise rapidly in them. Most people, however, find their desires and needs inadequately fulfilled in bureaucracies. Particularly common is the feeling of being manipulated and at the mercy of impersonal forces, even though the people at the top of the bureaucracy may have been elected to their positions by popular vote and can be removed by proper procedures. As a result, there frequently grows up within the formal structure of the bureaucratic organization an informal structure which provides ways of circumventing the rules, of expediting services, of obtaining special privileges, of gaining access to information on the lower levels that properly should be confined to higher levels so that future events may be anticipated, and, in general, of controlling one's own destiny.

The informal structures that grow up inside bureaucracies are primary groups. Since almost everybody has had experience living in the family, it is not surprising that they enter into the same kind of relationships outside the family whenever they can. The impersonal production line of the factory is controlled by primary groups of workers who mutually agree to restrict their output. Girls in mechanized offices form intimate cliques. High school students seek prestige among their peers by assuming the peer group's values, rather than satisfying the school bureaucracy's ends by getting good grades. Informal political structures—ward machines—arise to give people information about and access to the political bureaucracy.

Many directors of bureaucracies, having become aware of how important primary group contacts are to people, deliberately stimulate the formation of primary groups. Factory managers who do this are often rewarded by an increase in production and a decrease in absenteeism and grievances. To lessen the impact of bureaucracy, large universities sometimes provide family-type residences for their students and often divide entering students into small groups which stay together during the period of orientation.

When voluntary associations are successful and become nation wide in membership, they frequently turn into bureaucracies. Even so, they usually have local chapters, some of which are primary groups. Some individuals turn voluntary associations into primary groups for themselves by devoting their whole lives to the group. For a great many people voluntary associations are something in between a primary and a secondary group. Contacts are intimate, although less so than in the family, and the individual often finds meaningful goals for himself in the work of the group. This is one aspect of socialization. The kindergarten class is a good example of a group which is less primary than the family, but does have some of the characteristics of a primary group.

COMMUNICATION

There are still further ways a sociologist can look at social phenomena. During the process of socialization, people are communicating with one another. Starting from this observation, sociologists have discovered that groups can be divided into those in which the members communicate with each other and those in which they do not. There are relatively few of the latter and almost all human groupings fall into the first category. Sociologists summarize these observations by saying that *social life is the result of communication and interaction.* A *society* or *integrated group* is any group of people interacting and communicating among themselves. Most sociologists do not think of a society solely as a large city or nation. A family is a society, so is a class of students, the National Educational Association, a hospital ward, or a boy's gang. On the basis of size, permanency, and other characteristics, sociologists distinguish groupings of people by the terms "group," "organization," and "institution." Each of these types, however, is a society or communicating group.

A family is a society because the family members talk to each other and mutually adjust their behavior (interact). When junior and sister and father all want the car at the same time, they must make demands, justify their demands, try to see the others' points of view, and come to some decision. They do not have to agree. They may get angry. They may hate each other, but they do interact and communicate with each other.

Communication among members of the National Educational Association is not necessarily face to face and intimate, but it exists. To become a member one has to send in dues. In return one receives the literature of the group and is notified of policies and meetings one may attend and participate in. The degree of participation among the members may vary enormously. Some people pay dues and do nothing else for the group, while others may devote most of their lives to furthering the aims of the group. In both cases there is some communication with other members of the group.

In contrast, window-shoppers do not communicate with each other at all, either by word or gesture. People may bump into one another without either getting angry or apologizing. If an accident should occur on the street and the passers-by stop to help, a society might develop. A person trained in first aid might assume charge and direct others. There might be argument and discussion as to the best thing to do. Communication and interaction would occur. Such a society is, of course, ephemeral and is of less interest to sociologists than a universal and basic group like the family. The formation of a society out of a casual crowd does illustrate that the mere grouping together or aggregating of people does not produce a society. Communication must be present.

Crowds, Audiences, and Publics

When communication does not occur among group members, we speak of *nonintegrated* groups, and some of these are becoming increasingly important in modern society. A group of window-shoppers is called a *casual crowd*. A group of people wildly excited but not communicating with each other—as the spectators at a football match or people fleeing in panic from a theater fire—is called an *expressive crowd*. If someone can make himself heard in a panicked crowd and establish communication between himself and the crowd members, he can turn an expressive crowd into a society, which can take deliberate and sensible common action.

A third kind of crowd is the *acting crowd*—a lynch mob or a group of rioters. Once a crowd begins to form, communication ceases. Members of the crowd respond to the physical nearness of others, the commonly generated excitement, meaningless shouts and noises. Again, if somebody can re-establish communication before the crowd begins to act, a society emerges, and mob action never takes place. Police are trained in methods of turning a crowd into a society.

The people listening to a TV program also are not a society. They are responding individually to a common stimulus—the program. If they do not ever communicate with each other, they are called an *audience*. If the program is, let us say, a broadcast of a national political convention and people discuss it with their friends and acquaintances next day or write letters to the newspapers about what transpired, we call the group a *public*. A public is a large, informal discussion group and provides indirect communication among its members, usually through the mass media. A public is thus in some respects like an integrated group, although it resembles nonintegrated groups as well.

Sociologists do not make these distinctions on the basis of whether or not there is communication among group members because of a desire for hair-splitting precision. The absence of communication among the members of a group has severe and usually undesirable consequences. Those that follow the formation of an expressive or acting crowd are obvious. The effect of having many audiences in a society is not so clear.

If people do not communicate with each other but respond only to an outside stimulus, they lose the ability to communicate. For the individual this may mean mental illness just as if he were locked up away from people. Democracy cannot exist in a nation in which people engage largely or entirely in audience behavior instead of communicating with one another, either directly or indirectly.

Mass Society

George Orwell's novel *1984* portrays a *mass* society, one in which the members are completely manipulated through propaganda directed to audiences through the mass media. Nazi Germany was a mass society; many Communist countries are almost mass societies. Sociologists regard anything that breaks down communication as dangerous to democracy, and this is why they are concerned about the extent to which people watch TV or are spectators at sports rather than active participants in groups.

In the past year (1964) the newspapers have reported several occasions in which bystanders refused to go to the aid of women being attacked. In one case people were watching through their windows and had access to telephones, but, out of thirty-five spectators, only one called the police and then not until almost an hour had passed. In another case, the attack took place in a crowded office building, and the woman called repeatedly for help. These examples of audience rather than participant or interacting behavior worry sociologists more than crime or changes in values.

In a large, heterogeneous society such as most modern societies are, communication throughout the whole society is difficult to maintain. The mass media—radio, newspapers, magazines, and TV—can spread common information over a wide area. The transformation of this information into common values and meanings depends on the way groups are structured and the extent to which people participate in them.

The establishment of many publics, largely by permitting free communication, is one way of combatting audience behavior. Another is the proliferation of voluntary associations which, by informing and orienting their members in a mass society, enable them to control their destinies by rational collective action.

Since communication seems to be a key or distinguishing characteristic of many groups, sociologists have tried to analyze and find out more about it. While some communication takes place by signs and gestures, it is immediately apparent that almost all human communication is verbal and proceeds from *mind* to *mind*. This has prompted sociologists to say that society exists in the minds of its members. Modern sociology is based firmly on the assumption that a society needs neither a geographic base nor artifacts (material things) to exist but consists of the *sum* of the *ideas* held by all the individuals who make up a group.

This is a very difficult thing to comprehend, and yet it is one of the most essential elements of the sociological perspective. It is difficult to think of the United States without thinking of its territory spreading from ocean to ocean, its farms and cities, its schools and factories, its automobiles and airplanes. If, however, Americans suddenly disappeared, leaving intact all their material possessions, there would be no society. Conversely, if a large group of Americans were stranded in a remote place, there is no doubt that, within the physical possibilities available, they would recreate a society organized around prevailing American values.[4]

When a teacher thinks of "my class," she probably thinks of it within a specific classroom having certain books, maps, and other artifacts at its disposal. But the class exists only when the members and the teachers are communicating with each other. When class is dismissed the group ceases to exist until all are assembled again. Each member carries part of the class in his mind, and it takes all the minds together to make the class.

Not only do sociologists find it necessary to think of society as existing in the minds of its members in order to get a clear picture of what society is, but there are also practical reasons for maintaining this point of view. For example, statistical analysis shows that juvenile delinquency, alcoholism, family disorganization, and other unpleasant phenomena occur more frequently in blighted and run-down neighborhoods of the city than they do in better-kept residential areas. With the best intentions in the world, Americans jumped to the conclusion that, if the facilities of blighted areas were improved or if the residents were moved to other neighborhoods, these social problems would disappear. Despite the expenditure of billions of dollars on low-cost housing and urban renewal, neither of these solutions has worked. Disorganized families are just as disorganized in bright, new housing projects as they were in the slums, because they carry their society with them in their minds.

When urban renewal was started and the blighted areas examined one by one, so that their individual characteristics were not lost in statistical averages, it was found that many of the neighborhoods were highly organized. The residents, far from suffering from social problems, were happy and able to mobilize themselves to oppose destruction of their neighborhoods. Again, the significant fact was the ideas in the minds of people and not the external aspects of the neighborhoods.

---

[4]William Golding's novel, *Lord of the Flies* (London: Faber, 1954), illustrates this well. A group of English boys, stranded on an island, established exactly the kind of primitive, violent society one would expect of half-socialized young males. The English naval officer who rescued them said, "Bad show for English boys." As a fully socialized adult, he had very different ideas of what constitutes a "good society."

CULTURE

The location of society in the minds of its members does not simplify the task of sociologists. What goes on in the minds of individuals cannot be directly observed. It can only be inferred from external behavior—from the way in which an individual behaves either toward

1. objects (what their meaning is to him) or
2. other people (the nature of his interactions).

The most frequently observed external behavior is verbal—what a person says he thinks or believes or wants or dislikes or what he says to another person. On page 44 the description of what goes on in the mind of the small child during socialization is an example of this kind of analysis.

But sociologists also try to find out what is going on in the minds of all the people of a group. They are concerned about the meanings and values that are *shared* by group members. This can be stated as follows: *A culture consists of the shared meanings and values that the members of any group hold in common.* Culture is acquired through the interaction and communication that goes on among the members of a group.

A *meaning* is similar to a dictionary definition and tells people how to behave toward an object. The usual meaning of the word "chair" is "something to sit on." Of course, a chair can have many meanings. It can also be "the antique I inherited from my grandmother," "something to kick at when angry," or, to a child at play, "the engine of my train." Meanings vary from group to group. An automobile may mean convenient transportation to suburbanites, independence and prestige to teenagers. In the United States a bicycle is used for recreation, mainly by young people. In an underdeveloped country, it may mean wealth and power to the owner. In some European countries a bicycle is a means of adult transportation. The bicycle, the artifact, does not vary; the meaning of it does.

A *value* is any attitude which has some positive or negative emotion connected with it. Some values are commonly accepted by a group, but failure to conform to these values does not arouse much excitement. Although it is customary for women to wear a hat to a Protestant church service and most women do, someone otherwise properly dressed would cause little comment if she went hatless to church. Other values are strongly held, and, if they are violated, the violator may be gossiped about, ostracized, or deprived of public esteem.

Public esteem is also bestowed on individuals in order to encourage desirable behavior. Occasionally a school will award letters for scholarship as they do for excellence in athletics in an attempt to increase the public esteem awarded to bright students. This device may not always work, but it indicates that most people are aware of the social function of public esteem.

Some values the group regards as essential for its welfare. These are called *mores* and there are not many of them in a modern society. Today in the United States, our mores forbid such things as incest, cannibalism, and treason. For the most part, people do not violate the mores, and if they do the group's disapproval is immediate, spontaneous, and violent. Theoretically, the values of any group can be arranged along a continuum with those least strongly held at one end and the mores at the other.

When a country has many groups in it, each with its own set of meanings and values (as has the United States), social change is inevitable. Individuals belong to many groups and thus acquire and hold simultaneously different and sometimes conflicting values which they must somehow reconcile. The values of whole groups of people are given expression by their leaders and other spokesmen and become known and debated through the mechanism of the public. Thus, pluralistic societies have one kind of social change built into them. Only in isolation can a group maintain its culture unchanged.

The white Southerner's belief in the segregation of whites and Negroes is a strongly held value, but it is changing. Large numbers of white Southerners have gone into the racially integrated armed services, have gone North to work or to school. There they have been exposed to a different set of values about the capacities of the Negro and his place in society. Industrialization of the South has brought Northerners to live there, and they have carried their ideas into the South. Television, radio, and the mass circulation magazines have exposed Southerners to new ideas. As a result of the breakdown of Southern isolation, the old value system of the South is fast disappearing. The reader should note that this discussion of how values change answers some of the questions about consensus raised in Chapter 2, page 18.

Culture is not a miscellaneous collection of meanings and values. Meanings and values cluster together and are called roles. When we met the concept of role before, we were looking at it from the point of view of an individual. From this perspective, role was seen as a pattern of behavior directed, in the form of expectations, from one person to another and accepted as a guide to behavior.

From another perspective, a group can be thought of as a complex of roles. The family, for example, can be thought of as the combined roles of father, mother, wife, husband, parent, son, daughter, child, brother, and sister. To these we can add such roles as henpecked husband, career woman, nagging wife, philandering husband, devoted daughter, and the myriad of others one can think of.

Within any group the members evaluate group roles differently. A leader is more highly regarded than a rank-and-file member, and members must have certain qualities before they can become leaders. Mothers are evaluated differently than fathers or brothers and sisters. Each role complements all other roles so that the totality of roles in any group forms a functioning whole.[5] A school has those who learn as well as those who teach, those who supervise and direct as well as those who look after the health of the students or who clean up the building. Each of the individuals who fill these roles has some position (status) in the group relative to all other members of the group. Every role thus has a status attached to it, and some sociologists speak of status-role instead of role.

From the point of view of the group, role conflict also takes on new dimensions. Some role conflicts are solved by developing a new role which synthesizes elements of the old conflicting roles. When this happens in a major social role, the structure of the group can be changed. The changing roles of women affect the basic structure of the family and permanently alter the relationships among family members. The altering of relationships among people is what is meant by *role change*.

Sociologists have concepts other than role which can be used to analyze culture. They abstract out *systems of meanings and values* and call them *ideologies*. All the phrases that are used to justify American democracy and all the behavior Americans as citizens are expected to engage in or refrain from doing form the democratic ideology. Groups have *symbols* [6] which stand for the

---

[5] Remember that we are talking about patterns of behavior and not individuals. If a family has no mother, the father or an older sister or an outsider may play the role, or they may share it. If no one plays a major role in the group, the group is described as disorganized to at least some degree.

[6] A very easy to read and enlightening book about symbols in a mass society is Orrin E. Klapp, *Symbolic Leaders: Public Dramas and Public Men* (Chicago: Aldine Publishing Co., 1964).

meanings and values of the ideology, as the American flag stands for democracy. Part of an ideology consists of *myths* which illustrate and explain an ideology. The myth that "anybody can be President" is a shorthand way of saying that we have a free society without rigid class lines. One learns an ideology in the same way one learns a role—through internalizing the expectations directed toward one by a group. When children recite the "Pledge of Allegiance" in a classroom they are performing a *ritual* before a *symbol* of the *ideology* of American democracy. This is one way they learn the ideology. When a child who belongs to the Jehovah's Witnesses refrains from reciting the "Pledge," he experiences role conflict and is in the middle of an ideological conflict.

SOCIAL PROCESSES

A final perspective from which sociologists analyze societies focuses on the social act. Earlier in the chapter we described the simplest kind of social act, the unit of interaction, when we recounted what goes on when a parent directs expectations to a child and the child constructs a response. When one social act follows another and depends upon or proceeds from the prior act, sociologists speak of a *social process*. Interaction, either between or among individuals or between or among groups, occurs in the form of social processes. Sociologists have found that the *kinds of relationships among groups and among group members are universal and recurrent*. There are hundreds of social processes, but some are far more important than others.

Everywhere children are born into families and learn the ways of their society. They undergo *socialization*. Nations go to war with each other; children in the nursery fight; and the Democrats try to defeat the Republicans at election time. In all three cases *conflict* is occurring. Students in a class vie for grades, and businessmen try to win customers from each other. Both the students and the businessmen are engaging in *competition*.

The social process of conflict is second in importance only to socialization. Conflict is a basic social process because by engaging in conflict with each other, groups determine their relationships, one to another. A stable, organized society controls conflict. It limits it with rules of the game. Political conflict in the United States is a good example of this. It takes place by persuasion and propaganda, not by violence. The losers accept their defeat, and the winners restrain their vengeance. Collective bargaining between labor and industry is another example of limited conflict. A large amount of conflict is channeled through the courts.

After conflict has ended, new relationships may be established. The union may have gained recognition and more power in the economic system. The Republicans may have control of the political system. After race riots the Negroes' rights have frequently been recognized and guaranteed. Conflict is thus one of the major ways in which social change takes place.

Traditional societies are stratified into classes or castes, some of which have more power than others. Shifts of power occur only through conflict among the classes, as in the Cuban revolution led by Castro. In an open-class society such as ours, conflict is often replaced by competition. Individuals and groups vie with one another for identical goals. The progress of one impedes the progress of another, but there is no personal antagonism toward or, possibly even identification of, the competitors. Individuals and groups compete with each other for better education or for more money or for power and prestige. The ability to control valued items can thus move from individual to individual and from group to group without conflict.

If space permitted, it would be possible to list other important sociological insights. Those we have chosen for this chapter fit together into a systematic, integrated theory, along with the other material presented in the earlier parts of the book, to which we have sometimes referred in footnotes.

The necessity of compressing a great deal of material into a brief space has resulted in a presentation which seems more systematic than it really is. Conflicts among sociologists, ambiguities, and the problem of lack of sufficient empirical proof have not been presented. Nevertheless, the author feels that this chapter does present a comprehensive and balanced description of modern sociological theory.

Current Research in Sociology

chapter six

In previous chapters research results have often been described very briefly for the purpose of illuminating theory. In the section on methodology, highly artificial research designs were discussed to make clear the scientific process. This chapter describes some recent pieces of research in all their imperfection and with all their limitations to give the reader a more realistic idea of current research.

No claim is made that the studies here described are representative in any way of the total amount of research being produced. Everything described is considered by the writer to be good research, but so are hundreds of other studies not included. The choice of these pieces is biased in a number of ways: First, the author could consider only the research she knew about. It is impossible for anybody to read all that comes out. Secondly, book-length research reports were found to be too detailed to describe in a few paragraphs and are under-represented. Finally, much good research is addressed to technical problems that cannot be explained quickly to the layman, and other findings require some mathematical competence to understand. These kinds of research were omitted. On the other hand, research described in general books of readings predominates. Since other sociologists have thought well enough of the research to report it, the choice of these studies as "good" and representative does not depend on the judgment of one person.

The author wishes to offer a word of apology for the classifications of the research. Since the studies were not chosen to represent any subject or theory, the classification came after the pieces were chosen. The categories under which the research is examined are meant merely to provide a frame of reference for the reader.

SOCIALIZATION

As one would expect of a science interested in socialization, much research has been done on children and adolescents. The most systematic work has been done by Jean Piaget, a Swiss social psychologist. All his research has been done at the *Institut Jean Jacques Rousseau* in Geneva and covers a period of more than forty years. Piaget has been interested in the way intellectual understanding and a sense of morality develop. He has a series of experiments which indicate that the small child's perceptions of the material world are very different from those of older children and adults. The experiments by which he demonstrates this are extremely ingenious.

Piaget has shown that if a short, squat glass and a long, thin glass are placed on a table and water poured from the short glass into the long glass, small children will say that the tall glass has more water in it because the water level is higher. Even when the children see the water poured back and forth and their attention is called to the fact that the quantity of the water is the same, they persist in their beliefs. Similarly, they think there is more clay in a piece rolled out into a long, thin strip than in the ball from which it was rolled, even though the process is reversed before their eyes again and again. At some point in experience, however, the child grasps the idea of the conservation of matter. Older children immediately know that the amount of water and clay is the same and cannot be shaken from their conviction.

In another experiment, Piaget had a very large relief map of the Alps placed on a table. Standing at different places on the map were small dolls. The children were asked how the mountains would appear to the various dolls. Young children answered that the dolls would see the same thing as they (the children) did. They were incapable of grasping that what is seen varies with the position one takes. Older children had no difficulty in grasping the concept at once.

These and many other experiments demonstrate that what we regard as common sense is not a "given" but is the result of experience. They help us understand why children who are isolated or deprived of experiential opportunities fail to develop mentally. Teachers who worked with "culturally deprived" children found empirically that these children had not had a "normal" experience with language. Exposed to it in special pre-school classes, they were thereafter able to keep up with their peers. Piaget's experiments give us a more detailed understanding of the effect experience has on learning.

Another interest of Piaget is how children acquire the moral values of a society. He wanted to give specificity to such statements as: "Children are taught moral values by their parents, teachers, and peers." He observed Swiss children playing marbles and asked a number of them (about twenty) to explain the rules to him. Very young children followed no rules but played any way they wanted to. At a slightly older age, children sometimes followed rules, as they thought they had observed others do, but they did not compete with each other. At this stage they think the rules are absolute and have always existed. Older children play a socialized game with intricate rules. They understand the rules and argue about which rules should apply. They agree that the rules could be changed if everybody agreed to the change. Piaget points out that the play of young children is "egocentric" as compared to the "socialized," later stage which takes the behavior of others into account.

Mead and other social psychologists have been interested in children's play because it occurs universally. Mead felt that play was one of the major socializing processes. In acting out realistic roles such as mother, teacher, or policeman, the child is rehearsing adult roles he may some day play. In acting out imaginary roles such as cowboy or spaceman, the child is rehearsing desirable or undesirable (from society's point of view) attitudes, behaviors, and values of a complexity that does not occur in his daily life. Mead did no research on children's play, but Piaget's observations on marble play bear out Mead's theories. Children's attitudes on game rules are a rehearsal for their attitudes toward broader social rules, and they develop during interaction.

Piaget's theories do not rest on these observations alone. He devised a series of pairs of stories. In one story of each pair, the child *accidentally* does something wrong. In one, a little girl cuts a large hole with scissors; in another, a boy breaks fifteen cups. In the matching stories, the child *deliberately* misbehaves but with less serious consequences. The little girl makes a small hole; the boy breaks only three cups. Young children feel that the children who caused the most damage are the naughtier. Older children judge intent. Piaget felt that the shift in moral understanding was the result of becoming able to set one's self apart from others and to imagine one's self into their minds and understand their intent.

There have been other studies of how morality develops in children, some confirming Piaget, others, not. Some of the difference is due to what was studied, some to the methods used, and some to cultural differences among the children. Although there is still much to learn about how moral standards are internalized and how the mind develops, much credit must go to Piaget for pioneering systematic research and for inventing ingenious techniques for studying children.[1]

Kenneth B. and Mamie P. Clark[2] did an interesting study on how awareness of one's race affected American Negro children. They tested two groups of children, aged three to seven years, one group from a segregated school system in the South, the other from racially mixed schools in Massachusetts. The children were given four dolls, alike except for their color. The experimenter then asked children to:

1. Give me the doll that you like to play with.
2. Give me the doll that is a nice doll.
3. Give me the doll that looks bad.
4. Give me the doll that is a nice color.
5. Give me the doll that looks like a white child.
6. Give me the doll that looks like a colored child.
7. Give me the doll that looks like a Negro child.
8. Give me the doll that looks like you.

The study showed that almost all the children were aware of racial identification and chose the proper doll when asked to make the distinction among the white and colored dolls. The older the child, the more likely he was to know the term, "Negro," and the more likely he was to choose a colored doll when asked to present a doll which resembled him. There were no significant differences between northern and southern children in these respects. The majority of the children preferred the white doll and disliked the colored doll, although this preference decreased with age. The study indicates that racial awareness and racial preferences develop at a very early age. That some strain is present is indicated by the following quotation from the study:

> . . . some of the children . . . broke down and cried or became somewhat negativistic . . . when they were required

---

[1] Piaget has written more than twenty-five books and 160 articles. A sympathetic and penetrating analysis of the Genevan research can be found in Roger Brown, *Social Psychology* (New York: The Free Press, 1965), 195–245, 322–28, 340–42, 402–10.

[2] "Racial Identification and Preference in Negro Children," in Eleanor Maccoby, Theodore M. Newcomb, and Eugene L. Hartley, editors, *Readings in Social Psychology* (New York: Holt, Rinehart & Winston, Inc., 1958), 602–11.

to make self indentifications . . . A northern five-year-old dark child felt compelled to explain his identification with the brown doll by making the following unsolicited statement: "I burned my face and made it spoil." A seven-year-old northern light child went to great pains to explain that he is actually white but: "I look brown because I got a suntan in the summer." [3]

There have been other investigations of the effect of the caste system on the self concepts and attitudes of Negro children and adolescents which show that negative white attitudes are often internalized to the detriment of the self respect and ambition of the minority children.

For some time it has been recognized that the educational system is structured in harmony with middle-class values and that it inculcates these values, both directly and subtly. Sociologists have wondered about the impact of a middle-class education upon children with lower-class home cultures. One of the most interesting studies was done in London and then repeated in the United States.[4]

The researchers studied six hundred 13- to 14-year old English boys in the state schools. A great deal of information was collected for each child, including his school performance, his value system, his awareness of class differences, his performance on personality tests, and other relevant data. It was found that middle class children were more concerned about how well they do at school, more integrated into the school, and had higher educational and vocational aspirations. Although the middle class children had more rigid value systems, were less interested in the opposite sex, and were generally subjected to greater pressures, they were no more anxious or tense than lower class boys.

The researchers had hypothesized that the upwardly socially mobile working class boy would try to become middle class in his values and would differ from the working class boy who was not socially mobile. This hypothesis was proved. Not only did the socially mobile working class boy differ markedly from other working class boys, but his parents held more middle class values than did the parents of middle class boys.

It was also found that the teachers, when asked to pick the five best and five worst children, chose as best those children who most clearly exhibited middle class habits. The more upwardly mobile the teacher, the more she was likely to do this.

---

[3] *Ibid.*, 611.

[4] Hilde T. Himmelweit, "Socio-economic Background and Personality," in E. P. Hollander and Raymond G. Hunt, editors, *Current Perspectives in Social Psychology* (New York: Oxford University Press, 1963), 132–36.

Mr. J. Montague administered the same questionnaires to seven hundred boys of the same age in Spokane, Washington. Preliminary analysis of these questionnaires showed that the English and American middle classes have more in common with one another than do the working and middle classes in either country.

One form of socialization is professionalization. Adults who enter into law, medicine or other professions have to acquire not only the necessary skills but also the attitudes and values of the profession. The two studies we report on below demonstrate two different ways of studying professionalization.

Donald P. Irish[5] was interested in the extent to which the ancient Hippocratic oath was still being administered to young doctors. He asked about this in eighty-four American medical colleges. Twenty-six per cent did not utilize any oath. Of those which administered some oath, seven per cent used the Hippocratic oath, fourteen per cent used a modernized version of it, eleven per cent gave an international oath known as the Geneva oath, and thirty per cent used some other oath. Irish analyzed the elements of the oaths. He found that although they varied widely, several important themes were always included. These were: (1) the welfare of patients as a prime concern; (2) the protection of privacy and confidentiality; (3) avoidance of injury and wrong; and (4) the sacredness of human life.[6]

A survey like Irish's gives a broad picture of one aspect of socialization—the explicit indoctrination of the values a profession considers important. Another way of learning how professional values are acquired is exemplified in a study by Howard S. Becker and Blanche Geer.[7] These researchers were participant observers in a state medical school. They took part in all the classes and other activities and got to know the students well.

Although Becker and Geer studied many other aspects of professionalization, in this article they examine how the amorphous idealism of the entering freshman is molded into a more realistic and effective idealism by the time of graduation. The first two years of medical school are so extremely demanding that students have no time for idealism. During the last two years, the students

---

[5] "Professional Oaths and American Medical Colleges," *Journal of Chronic Diseases,* 18 (1965), 275–89.

[6] In private conversation, Professor Irish says he has been deluged with requests for this article from medical schools, here and abroad, indicating the medical profession's concern with its ethical code.

[7] "The Fate of Idealism in Medical Schools," *American Sociological Review,* 23 (1958), 50–56.

deal directly with patients. To the lay observer, they may seem cynical, but in reality they are only preoccupied with technical details. The observers say that, underneath, the students are still idealistic. When issues of idealism are openly raised, students respond as before, but there is not much time to discuss such things. Seniors show more interest in serious ethical dilemmas of the kind they expect to face in practice. The authors sum it up as follows:

> . . . as school comes to an end, the cynicism specific to the school situation also comes to an end and their [the students'] original and more general idealism about medicine comes to the fore again, though within a framework of more realistic alternatives. Their idealism is now more informed although no less selfless.[8]

CONFLICT OF VALUES

Rapid change and a multiplicity of sub-groups are important characteristics of modern society. Conflicts of values thus often occur within the society. In *An American Dilemma*, Myrdal suggested that some values are "higher" than others; that is, the members of the society regarded these values as higher or better. He argued that the higher values, which he subsumed under the term the "American Creed," would prevail if a choice were forced. Presented as a general explanation of social behavior, this theory was specifically applied to racial attitudes in *An American Dilemma*. Myrdal did not try to test his theory. Although there has been a great deal of research on the relationship between attitudes and behavior, it remained for Frank R. Westie[9] to test Myrdal's theory directly in 1965. Westie gave questionnaires to 103 heads of households (or their spouses) in Indianapolis. The respondents were asked to indicate their degree of agreement with statements of general values derived from the American Creed. They were also asked how they would behave in a series of specific situations to which the general values could apply. Finally, the interviewers tried to find out what the subjects would say if there was a conflict between the general values they espoused and the behavior they would engage in in the specific situations.

Westie found considerable inconsistency between general values and behavior in specific situations. Some respondents recog-

---

[8] *Ibid.*, 55.
[9] "The American Dilemma: An Empirical Test," *American Sociological Review,* 30 (August, 1965), 527–38.

nized the discrepancy and tried to explain it away as Myrdal had predicted they would. Some refused to recognize the discrepancy even after the interviewer pointed it out to them. Westie found that the rationalizations used to harmonize the discrepancies were of a variety of kinds contrary to Myrdal's theory that they would call upon a general held cultural belief to justify their statements. Westie did find, however, that almost eighty-two per cent of the "explanations" of discrepancies were adjustment of behavior in the specific situation to the American Creed values giving general support to Myrdal's thesis.

An interesting finding was that those who both espoused the American Creed values and indicated behavior *harmonious* with these values often found it necessary to justify their beliefs. This suggests that there is another set of widely held values about race not consonant with the American Creed values.

An interesting experiment on value conflict was done by Samuel Stouffer and Jackson Toby.[10] They asked people how they would react in situations of value conflict. In one situation a man, who had been riding with a friend who was arrested for speeding, is called upon to testify whether his friend was or was not going thirty-five miles an hour in a twenty-mile speed zone. He knows that his friend was speeding. He can testify for his friend and perjure himself, or commit perjury and support his friend. All the other situations require a similar choice—between supporting a friend or violating a social code.

The researchers concluded that each individual made consistent choices ranging from total support of the friend to total support of the social codes. If they knew the answer the respondent would give in one situation, they could accurately predict his other answers. In other words, each individual had a consistent way of judging right and wrong.

Kohlberg,[11] who studied children somewhat as Piaget did, presented them with complex moral dilemmas. He found stages in development as Piaget did, but his oldest children (seventeen years) argue from a generalized set of moral values much as the individuals in the Stouffer-Toby study do.

The most rigorous statement about conflict of values has been made by Leon Festinger in his theory of cognitive dissonance. Festinger argues that the attitudes of an individual normally are

---

[10] "Conflict and Personality," *American Journal of Sociology*, 56 (1951), 395–406.

[11] See Brown, *op. cit.*, 404–07, for a summary and analysis of Kohlberg's work.

consistent with each other and that he behaves in accordance with his attitudes. Whenever a person becomes aware that he is entertaining unharmonious or dissonant attitudes, he will try to reduce the dissonance and the accompanying psychological discomfort. A number of hypotheses have been deduced from the theory and tested.

One hypothesis is that if a person is pressured to say or do something contrary to his private attitudes. he will tend to modify his attitude to make it harmonious with what he has said or done. A corollary to this hypothesis is that the greater the pressure has been to act contrary to one's beliefs, the less the attitude will change.

To test this hypothesis[12] subjects who had just completed a dull and boring task were asked to explain to the next subject how enjoyable and exciting the experiment had been. Some subjects were offered one dollar for making this explanation, others were offered twenty dollars. After they had made the explanation, the subjects were interviewed and asked their opinions on the experiment. As was expected, those who had been paid one dollar rated the experiment more interesting than did those who had received twenty dollars. Both categories of subjects had been induced to change their attitudes for monetary rewards; the greater the pressure (as measured by the amount of payment), the less the change in attitude.

The Group Dynamicists, of whom Festinger is one, have been leaders in conducting their experiments under fairly rigorous laboratory conditions. At times they have been criticized on the grounds that they do not know what population their volunteer or paid subjects represent. One of their studies, however, deals with the theory of cognitive dissonance in a natural group.

The investigators[13] joined a small religious sect whose members believed in the imminent end of the world. Their leader had predicted the date on which it would occur. On the appointed night the group gathered to await the end. When the hour of doom came and went but the world continued, the group was at first extremely depressed. Soon, however, the leader of the group produced another message which explained the failure of the cataclysm to occur. The group eagerly accepted this. They talked willingly to newspapermen and tried to win converts in the following weeks.

---

[12] Leon Festinger and J. M. Carlsmith, "Cognitive Consequences of Forced Compliance," *Journal of Abnormal and Social Psychology*, 58 (1959) 203–10.
[13] Leon Festinger, Henry W. Riecken and Stanley Schachter, "When Prophecy Fails," in Maccoby, Newcomb and Hartley, *op. cit.*, 156–63.

A few members of the group were college students who had gone home during the time predicted for the world to end. They were isolated from the main part of the group and their behavior was different. They lost their faith and tried to hide the fact that they had been members of the group.

The events supported the original hypothesis that disconfirmation of a deeply held belief would intensify the belief and encourage proselytizing—provided that the believers had social support. The failure of the isolated students to continue their beliefs confirms the hypothesis that social support is necessary to support beliefs that fail.

STUDIES IN NATURAL SETTINGS

Researchers like to study attitudes and behavior in realistic settings when possible, as was done in the study just described. One of the best places to do such studies is in the Armed Forces because once a study is approved, it is relatively easy to get an adequate sample to study.

Today the Armed Forces are racially integrated, but they were not during most of World War II. On an experimental basis, a number of all-Negro platoons were introduced into white infantry companies with white officers and white non-commissioned officers. Sometime later, members of the Research Branch[14] of the Information and Education Division, War Department, interviewed a cross section of members of seven of the eleven integrated divisions. Two of the divisions were predominantly Southern in background. Interviews revealed very favorable attitudes toward the Negro troops, particularly in combat. Many interviewees were doubtful, however, about integration in a garrison situation. Officers, when interviewed, testified that relations among the men had been good, and there had been no difficulty although many of them had anticipated trouble.

Probably the most interesting finding was that the closer men come to the integrated situation, the less opposition they had to it. Men actually in a company with a Negro platoon were most favorable to it; those in units without a Negro platoon were least favorable.

Housing projects also provide a useful site for research projects. One of the most interesting of these was a study comparing the

---

[14] Shirley A. Star, Robin Williams, Jr., and Samuel A. Stouffer, "Negro Infantry Platoons in White Companies" in *ibid.*, 596–601.

changes in racial prejudice in two housing projects.[15] One project was integrated; in the other, Negro and white families lived in the same project but were in separate buildings. The projects were roughly similar; both had about the same percent of Negroes living in them; all the families were from similar, low-income groups; the neighborhoods surrounding the projects were much the same.

The housewives in the project were interviewed about their racial attitudes. Although most of the white housewives in the integrated projects had not liked the idea of living in the same building with Negroes when they moved in, they had acquired much more favorable attitudes toward Negroes. They also had many friendly inter-family contacts with the Negro families. The change was even more pronounced among the children. On the other hand, tenants in the segregated units had not changed their attitudes. The similarity of results in this and the preceding study is striking.

Another housing-project study compared the tenants of two projects in regard to their participation in and attitudes toward a tenants' council.[16] In one project, Westgate, the houses were arranged in U-shaped courts. In the other, Westgate, West, the apartments were in rows of two-story houses. Both projects were occupied by families of students of the Massachusetts Institute of Technology.

The authors hypothesized that group standards would form in the U-shaped project because the residents had greater access to each other. Common standards would be less likely to form in the row houses. They further hypothesized that where group standards were stronger, participation in the council would be greater and attitudes toward it more favorable. They were able to substantiate their hypotheses by the use of interviews in which they asked about the amount of participation in the council and how the residents felt about the council.

An American sociologist[17] in Italy was also able to make use of a housing project to compare the amount of social participation in two communities: one, an old, well-established, but run-down area; the other, a new, hastily thrown-together housing project.

15 Morton Deutsch and Mary Evans Collins, "The Effect of Public Policy in Housing Projects Upon Interracial Attitudes" in *ibid.*, 612–23.

16 Leon Festinger, Stanley Schachter, and Kurt Back, "The Operation of Group Standards," in Dorwin Cartwright and Alvin Zander, *Group Dynamics* (Evanston: Row, Peterson and Company, 1960), 241–59.

17 Arnold M. Rose, *Indagine Sull' Integrazione Sociale in Due Quartieri di Roma* (Rome: Istituto di Statistica, 1959).

Interviews in the homes, using a pre-formulated questionnaire, were conducted to compare the extent and pattern of social integration into the local community between the two housing areas. The members of the older community manifested greater integration into the local community, but there seemed no difference in the number of contacts with larger institutions such as churches, political parties, and voluntary associations. One of the major findings of this study demonstrated (for the first time) the feasibility of doing research in Italy using natural groups.

SMALL GROUPS

Simmel, writing in the early part of the twentieth century, had suggested that sociologists ought to study small groups. He felt that only in this way could the basic processes of interaction be properly understood. Since 1945 there has been a great revival of interest in the study of small groups, both inside and outside of the laboratory. While Simmel's hypotheses have not been neglected, the range of subjects investigated by studying small groups is multifarious. Unfortunately, it is hard to describe these pieces of research for the layman. Most of them are difficult and abstract. Two different studies will, however, be presented.

One of the interests of the small-group researchers has been to create experimentally a social condition or group atmosphere so that its effect on behavior may be studied free from distracting factors. One of the pioneering studies of this kind attempted to measure the differential effect of group atmosphere on children's aggressiveness.[18]

Four clubs of eleven-year old children were each subjected to different types of leadership over a seven-week period. Club leaders were instructed to act in an "authoritarian," "laissez-faire," or "democratic" manner. The kind of activities suitable for each type of leadership was set out in detail. The children in each group were similar in background factors, and each group experienced all three kinds of leadership. The accomplishments of the groups and the reactions of the boys were measured in a variety of ways.

The experiment clearly showed that it is possible to create a variety of group atmospheres by varying the type of leadership. In the laissez-faire group, less work and poorer work was done. More work was done in democratic groups, and quality was better.

---

[18] Ralph White and Ronald Lippitt, "Leader Behavior and Member Reaction in Three 'Social Climates'," in Cartwright and Zander, *op. cit.*, 527–53.

There was more play and more silliness in the laissez-faire group. More domination of one boy by another and far more hostility and aggressive demands occurred in the autocratic group than in the democratic group. Among other things it was found that the type of leadership determined both the pattern of social interaction and the emotional development of the group. For example, a group which had accepted an authoritarian leader at the first meeting was resistant to a second authoritarian leader after it had experienced a democratic leader.

In the Westgate study described earlier, the relative physical position of the residents affected their social relationships and thus their degree of participation in the community. There were, however, so many complicating factors that the role of physical position was obscured. Leavitt[19] has tried to study the effect of physical position in a laboratory situation in order to see its effect more clearly.

He arranged successive groups of subjects in four different positions—a circle, a wheel, a straight line, and a Y. Each group was asked to perform a simple task. Each member of the group was given a card with six different symbols on it, and their task was to find the symbol common to all cards in the group. It was found that the organization that developed for the purpose of settling the problem and the position at which leaders emerged varied with each pattern. The position of leader emerged most clearly in the wheel pattern, and this arrangement most often enabled its members to provide the quickest solution to the problem. The leaders enjoyed their work more than did other members of the group except in the circle, where all members enjoyed the task. While it is hard to know whether the results of this experiment could be extended to large groups, the results were so clear-cut, it is probably worth trying.

THE TESTING OF BASIC THEORY

Of all theories of how social life is carried on, George Herbert Mead's are among the most intellectually satisfying. In contrast to most other explanations, Mead's theories do not break social life down into the individual and the group, but he tries to explain

---

[19] Harold J. Leavitt, "Some Effects of Certain Communication Patterns on Group Performance," *Journal of Abnormal and Social Psychology*, 46 (1951), 38–50.

each in its relation with the other as observation shows them to be. He also avoids deterministic explanations and allows for the fact that men seem to be, or at least feel themselves to be, acting freely. Mead's theories, however, have been hard to test, and it is only recently that systematic testing of them has been tried.

Sheldon Stryker[20] meets Mead's challenge head-on. Mead states, among other things, that daily intercourse is possible because people share a set of common values and meanings arising from common group experience; they are, therefore, able to imaginatively predict what other people will do and to adjust to meet the expectations of others, a process Mead calls role-taking. Stryker had as subjects married adults and their parents, using a married couple and the parents of one, but not both. He provided his subjects with a self-administered interview schedule requiring attitude statements to which offspring and parents could respond for themselves and for one another. The schedule measured family ideology on an autocratic-democratic continuum. He found that the ability to predict varied a great deal. Prediction was more accurate about females than about males, when females did the predicting, when predictions were made about one's own relatives rather than about in-laws, and when predictions were made by one sex about the opposite sex. Stryker's conclusions were that Mead's theory is essentially sound and is testable by well-known means. He suggests, however, that the conditions under which accurate predictions occur and those factors which affect accuracy of prediction need to be studied in greater detail.

Another, more indirect, test of Mead's theory concerns the ability to predict what one's future role will be like. Mead assumes that social life takes place smoothly because there is a set of common expectations for behavior that extends into the future. Arnold M. Rose[21] tried to test whether young people had realistic future expectations about adult, female roles. He chose to study female roles because they are changing rapidly in our society.

Rose gave a questionnaire consisting of fifteen questions about expectations for adult roles to 256 University of Minnesota students. He found that almost all the women expected to raise children,

---

[20] "Conditions of Accurate Role-Taking: A Test of Mead's Theory," in Arnold M. Rose, editor, *Human Behavior and Social Processes* (Boston: Houghton Mifflin Company, 1962), 41–62.

[21] "The Adequacy of Women's Expectations for Adult Roles," *Social Forces*, 30 (October, 1951), 69–77.

spend a great deal of time on them and on housework. They almost all expected to get a job and also to be as active as men in leisure time work. The data indicated that the average woman wanted to and expected to play every kind of adult social role—a manifest impossibility both in terms of the time available and in terms of conflicting obligations. Rose concludes: "There is a certain inconsistency, lack of definiteness, and lack of realism about expectations for adult roles among a significant proportion of the women college students studied." This study, like the Stryker study, indicates that there is less smoothness, consistency, and predictability in social life than Mead's theories would indicate.

A study by Milton Rokeach and Louis Mezer[22] attempts to support the hypothesis that differences in belief on important issues are more powerful determinants of prejudice or discrimination than differences in race or ethnic membership. While this hypothesis does neglect the fact that race or ethnic membership may be the determinant of commonality of beliefs for most people, it does go to the Meadian proposition that social relationships depend upon mutual predictability of expectations.

In the Rokeach-Mezer experiments, a subject is engaged in group discussion with four strangers who are hired by the experimenter. Two of the confederates were white, two, Negro. One white and one Negro agree with the subject, and one white and one Negro disagree with him. This subject is then allowed to state or demonstrate his preference for two of the four confederates. Later he is asked his reason for the choice. Two experiments were performed: one in 1961 with twenty white, male students and one in 1963-64 with forty-eight white, male students.

On the basis of these experiments (and some others done a little differently), the authors conclude that "whatever racial attitudes our subjects may have had seem to have exerted little or no influence on actual choices in social situations where external pressures to discriminate along racial lines were slight or absent (and pressures *not* to discriminate along racial lines possibly present)." Choice seems to have been made on the basis of common values elicited in the discussion or of a favorable, general impression of the attitudes or personalities of the discussants. Thus, the set of common values and meanings seem to be of importance in the social choices made by the subjects in this study.

---

22 "Race and Shared Belief as Factors in Social Choice," *Science,* 151 (January, 1966), 167–72.

ACTION RESEARCH

Occasionally it is possible to set in motion an action program and then observe the results of the program. If the suggested action is based on an hypothesis derived from a theory, the results will either confirm or disprove the hypothesis and theory. A situation like this is the nearest approach to a *bona fide* experiment that the social scientist ever finds, and they are naturally on the lookout for such opportunities.

Lester Coch and John R. P. French, Jr.[23] did a piece of action research in a factory. The site was the main plant of the Harwood Manufacturing Corporation, a pajama manufacturing plant in Marion, Virginia. The management was unhappy because whenever they introduced necessary changes in production methods, the workers resisted them. The management asked help from Coch and French. The researchers theorized that resistance to change was in large part a result of group-induced forces. They proposed to try three different methods of introducing changes, each involving a different kind of group participation in the change-making decisions. This method enabled them to compare the results of different techniques of introducing change.

In the first variation, the employees were only given an explanation of the changes that would occur. The second group of workers elected representatives who helped design the changes and reported back to the group. In the third group, all members of the group met together with management and participated in designing the changes to be made in the job.

The results of the experiment showed that the greater the participation of workers in designing and planning for the change, the less resistance there was to change. The group members not only understood the reasons for the change and how they would be affected by them, but were able to suggest ways to make the changes less disorganizing. This experiment was repeated in a similar factory in Norway in 1956 with the same results.

Opportunities to do action research occur only rarely. They are more likely to occur in prisons, hospitals, or the Armed Forces where citizens have less than normal free choice. An interesting experiment was tried by George W. Fairweather.[24] He was con-

---

[23] "Overcoming Resistance to Change," in Maccoby, Newcomb and Hartley, *op. cit.*, 233–50.

[24] George W. Fairweather, editor, *Social Psychology in Treating Mental Illness: An Experimental Approach* (New York: John Wiley and Sons, 1964).

cerned with the problem of returning cured mental patients who had lived for a long time in a hospital to the larger community. Fairweather argued that usually a mental hospital is a closed community, and that the roles patients learn in the hospital are a handicap on the outside. He tried, therefore, to establish small groups of patients in the hospital and to release the groups as a whole, hoping that the relationships established within these groups would carry over outside and provide a transitional way of living.

His results indicated at least partial success. The small-group-treatment program reduced hospitalization and brought about more employment and active involvement with others. However, about fifty per cent of the patients had returned to the hospital within a period of six months.

The author feels that the research described in this chapter reveals a variety of very ingenious techniques for studying society. In every case a source is given so that the reader can find and read the complete report. It is hoped that this taste of sociological research will stimulate many readers to do exactly that.

Epilogue

The word root, *socius* (bond, tie, relationship), loosely translated, means "group." In English it also has the connotation of something good for the welfare of the group. We speak of social as opposed to asocial behavior. For this reason and because many sociologists study social problems, there is a widespread impression that sociologists are "do-gooders"—that their primary purpose is to do good. One sociologist has found it necessary in his introductory text to distinguish sociology from "socialism," an economic and political creed, and from "social work," a profession whose primary purpose *is* to alleviate social problems.

These misunderstandings crush sociologists who dearly wish to be recognized as scientists. It is hoped that this little book will have demonstrated that sociology is a science and a reasonably well-developed one. There is a very practical reason for recognizing that this is so. A science is value-free. Its findings can be used equally for good or evil purposes just as knowledge about the atom can be used to create bombs or to provide cheap industrial power. Sociologists are no better or worse than other men. They are of all political persuasions. They embrace as wide a range of values as any other group does. They can no more be depended upon to permit their findings to be used only for good ends than can the physicists be depended on not to provide the knowledge to make nuclear weapons.

Sociologists already control techniques that could be put to questionable uses. They know how to desocialize people (brainwashing). They know how to manipulate people through the mass media. They know how to build up or break down the morale of groups, a process that could be used by industry to destroy a union, for example, or by a corrupt national union leader to destroy an intransigeant local. It is important, therefore, that the

77

average citizen have some knowledge of the findings of sociology. He needs also to realize that it is the citizens of a democracy who must decide what values and policies should be implemented and not a group of scientists, no matter how reassuring the name of their profession is. Just as the findings of sociology can be put to evil uses, however, so can they be used to implement moral ends, as we have tried to indicate throughout this book.

Probably most of the members of any profession privately think their own profession superior to others. Somebody once called sociology, "the Queen of the Social Sciences." Although publicly sociologists repudiate this statement in the interests of harmony with their colleagues in the other sciences, privately most of us do believe that sociology *is* basic to all other social sciences. Whether it is or not, the findings of sociology should be known more widely. It is hoped that those who read this book will find sociology useful.

The writing of a book like this is, of course, a teaching effort. It has been both difficult and rewarding: difficult because communication is an art one never masters completely; rewarding because, as Henry Adams said, "A teacher affects eternity; he can never tell where his influence stops."

Appendices

Vocational Opportunities in Sociology

appendix one

Sociologists do one or a combination of the following things: teach; do research; or deal directly with people in an administrative, counseling, therapeutic, or advisory capacity. Usually a sociologist teaching at the university level, engaged in independent research, or supervising a large number of people must have his doctorate. There are numerous jobs in the field, however, that require only a bachelor's or master's degree.

TEACHING

The field with the largest number of jobs in sociology is, of course, teaching. To teach at a university or to do independent research requires an advanced degree, usually a Ph.D. Some two-year terminal or junior colleges now teach sociology, and a few high schools have sociology courses. If these trends continue, there will be many more teaching jobs for sociologists holding only the B.A. or M.A. degrees. Nursing schools, medical schools, and departments of social work and education often require their students to have sociology courses. They hire people with B.A. degrees in sociology or with combination degrees, since this task requires competence in more than the field of sociology and does not require a person trained to do sociological research.

CRIMINOLOGY

There are numerous uses for sociology in the field of criminology. Parole officers are frequently trained in sociology. Policemen, policewomen, and prison guards are often given in-service training by sociologists on juvenile delinquents and adult criminals and why they behave the way they do. In large cities in both the North and South, the police are frequently taught something about the problems of minority groups and how to get along in dissatisfied segregated communities without provoking incidents. A state or a large city will often hire its own sociologist to do this training. Superintendents of prisons, reformatories, and jails and the officers of juvenile courts and youth commissions are usually trained in criminology.

SPECIALISTS IN THE FAMILY

Churches, general and mental hospitals, public or private welfare agencies, schools, city, state, and federal park systems, unions, and industry hire sociologists specializing in the family. Sociologists serve as marriage counselors, give advice on children's problems, give vocational and legal advice to family members, operate programs for retired people, and plan recreational programs for adolescents for these agencies and institutions.

INTERGROUP RELATIONS

Most of the people working in the growing field of intergroup relations are trained in sociology. The staffs of the Fair Employment and the Fair Housing Practices Commissions are sociologists. Most northern and western states and many cities have commissions of this kind. The United States Employment Office, many federal agencies, employer's associations and large industries, advertising councils, and national unions are hiring minority group experts at an ever increasing rate. The defense organizations of minorities like the National Association for the Advancement of Colored People (NAACP) or the Anti-Defamation League of B'nai B'rith (ADL) have some sociologists on their staffs. Many national and international church organizations, newly concerned about race relations, are beginning to hire experts in the field.

COMMUNITY RELATIONS

Experts in community relations are finding new openings. Any organization which has to deal with community disruptions, such as agencies providing new housing or engaging in urban renewal, usually hire sociologists to help people through difficult transition stages. A number of projects are being conducted in disorganized communities in large cities to build the morale of the community and to encourage participation in community life. It is too early to assess the effectiveness of these projects, but if they are successful they will be copied all over the United States. Their staffs are composed partly of sociologists. Rural sociologists have served for a long time as community consultants both to well-organized and to depressed rural communities, and they have been very much in demand by UNESCO, other international agencies, and the U.S. State Department to work in underdeveloped countries. These countries are, of course, mostly rural and exhibit the kinds of problems with which rural sociologists are familiar.

EXPERTS ON PUBLIC OPINION

Many workers in public opinion are trained in sociology. This is one of the fastest growing fields of employment in the United States. Anyone interested in knowing the attitudes of a large section of the American public at any particular time and about any particular subject hires a public opinion expert. This kind of knowledge is useful to large industries and business associations, national unions, politicians and political parties, advertising agencies, newspapers, TV and radio chains. Sometimes this information is sold by businesses which specialize in taking polls, like the Gallup Poll. Sometimes universities or foundations have polling organizations which provide information about attitudes to scholars and research scientists. Polling organizations of both kinds hire many sociologists.

INDUSTRIAL SOCIOLOGY

Business, industry, and labor often hire sociologists. Many personnel directors are sociologists. The industrial sector of the economy supports much social research, some of it directed to specific problems, but much of it of general interest. A large part of this is sociological research.

MEDICAL SOCIOLOGY

Doctors and psychiatrists have become increasingly aware of the relevance of sociological findings to therapy. Medical research and new therapy is very often conducted by teams which include a sociologist along with medical and psychiatric personnel. Hospital administrators have found sociologists very useful in devising ways of raising morale among staff and patients.

DEMOGRAPHERS AND ECOLOGISTS

Some city planners are trained in ecology and hired by planning commissions. Demographers make up most of the enormous staff of the Census Bureau. Insurance firms hire population experts to make up actuarial tables on which insurance rates are based. Telephone companies, power companies, schools, or any group interested in the size of future populations hire demographers. International agencies also use them frequently.

FREE LANCING

Some sociologists free lance and offer their specialized services to firms which cannot afford to hire a full-time sociologist, much as some certified public accountants do. One sociologist told an investment firm he could, on the basis of his sociological knowledge, predict those areas in which the firm should invest, and that he would be satisfied with a percentage of the profits. Among other things, he told them (in 1945) to buy stock in a firm that manufactured school desks, on the basis of his knowledge of the increase in the birth rate and the inevitable increase in school-age children. He and the firm made a killing. This sounds simple, but apparently no one else thought of it!

Professional
Societies
and Learned
Journals

The American professional society to which most sociologists belong is the *American Sociological Association* (ASA). Its purpose is to maintain communication among sociologists to exchange and further knowledge in the field; to set up requirements for admission to the profession and to establish codes of ethics; to organize the job market; to serve as a liaison with government, industry, labor, and other social organizations; to maintain contact with sociologists in other countries. The official organ of the ASA is *The American Sociological Review,* the main purpose of which is to publish research and to keep sociologists informed about matters of professional interest to them. There are also regional and a few state associations which publish journals.

One of the results of the growth of sociology is increased specialization and a rapid accumulation of knowledge, creating the problem of how communication is to be maintained both among the practitioners within a specialty and among those in different specialties. To handle these problems sociologists form specialized associations. Although they are concerned with only a limited portion of the field, they perform for *their* members the same services as the ASA does for all sociologists. The specialized associations also publish journals.

In addition to the specialized sociological journals and the publications of the regional associations, some universities publish sociological journals. The oldest and best known of these is the *American Journal of Sociology,* published at the University of Chicago. Listed on page 111 are the major sociological societies and the most important sociological journals.

Association or University	Journal
American Sociological Association	*The American Sociological Review* and *Sociometry* and *Sociology of Education*
Ohio Valley Sociological Association	
Pacific Sociological Society	*The Pacific Sociological Review*
Eastern Sociological Society	
Southern Sociological Society	
Midwest Sociological Society	*Sociological Quarterly*
Southwest Sociological Society	*Southwestern Social Science Review*
District of Columbia Chapter of the ASA	
American Catholic Sociological Society	*American Catholic Sociological Review*
Rural Sociological Society	*Rural Sociology*
Society for the Study of Social Problems	*Social Problems*
University of Chicago	*The American Journal of Sociology*
Atlanta University	*Phylon*
University of North Carolina	*Social Forces*
University of Southern California	*Sociology and Social Research*
New School for Social Research	*Social Research*
Washington University (St. Louis)	*Trans-Action**
UNESCO	*International Sociological Bulletin*

* *Trans-Action* is a very readable journal and should be of particular interest to the layman.

A Selected List of Sociological References

The great increase of sociological knowledge has led to the establishment of *Sociological Abstracts,* a publication which abstracts and classifies most of the important research in sociology to provide a complete and accurate summary of what is being done in each field. In addition, there are a number of published summaries of research in various fields as well as books of readings which make available in convenient form research material first published in the learned journals. Some of the most useful of these are listed below. They can be found in any good-sized library.

GENERAL SOCIOLOGY

Index to the *American Sociological Review.* (Classifies by author and subject all articles and book reviews for the first 20 volumes.)

Borgatta, Edgar F., and Henry J. Meyer. *Sociological Theory: Present Day Sociology from the Past.* New York: Alfred A. Knopf, Inc., 1956.

Coser, Lewis A., and Bernard Rosenberg. *Sociological Theory: A Book of Readings.* New York: The Macmillan Co., 1957.

Gittler, Joseph B. *Review of Sociology: Analysis of a Decade.* New York: John Wiley & Sons, Inc., 1957.

Gurvitch, Georges, and Wilbert E. Moore (eds.). *Twentieth-Century Sociology.* New York: Philosophical Library, Inc., 1946.

Lipset, Seymour M., and Neil J. Smelser (eds.). *Sociology: The Progress of a Decade.* Englewood Cliffs, N.J.: Prentice-Hall, Inc., 1961.

Merton, Robert K., Leonard Broom, and Leonard S. Cottrell, Jr. (eds.). *Sociology Today: Problems and Prospects.* New York: Basic Books, Inc., Publishers, 1959.

Roucek, J. S. *Contemporary Sociology.* New York: Philosophical Library, Inc., 1958.

Schuler, Edgar A., *et al* (eds.). *Readings in Sociology.* 2nd ed. New York: Thomas Y. Crowell Co., 1960.

SOCIAL PSYCHOLOGY

Maccoby, Eleanor E., Theodore F. Newcomb, Eugene L. Hartley (eds.). *Readings in Social Psychology.* 3rd ed. New York: Holt, Rinehart & Winston, Inc., 1958.

Rose, Arnold M. (ed.). *Human Behavior and Social Processes: An Interactionist Approach.* Boston: Houghton Mifflin Co., 1962.

Stoodley, Bartlett H. (ed.). *Society and Self: A Reader in Social Psychology.* New York: Free Press of Glencoe, Inc., 1962.

SOCIAL STRUCTURE

Bendix, Reinhard, and Seymour Martin Lipset (eds.). *Class, Status and Power: A Reader in Social Stratification.* New York: Free Press of Glencoe, Inc., 1953.

Etzioni, Amitai (ed.). *Complex Organizations: A Sociological Reader.* New York: Holt, Rinehart & Winston, Inc., 1961.

Rose, Arnold M. (ed.). *The Institutions of Advanced Societies.* Minneapolis: University of Minnesota Press, 1958.

SOCIAL PROBLEMS

Lee, Elizabeth Briant, and Alfred McClung Lee (eds.). *Social Problems in America: A Source Book.* New York: Holt, Rinehart & Winston, Inc., 1955.

Merton, Robert K., and Robert A. Nisbet (eds.). *Contemporary Social Problems.* 2nd ed. New York: Harcourt, Brace & World, Inc., 1965.

SPECIAL SUBJECTS

Berelson, Bernard, and Morris Janowitz. *Reader in Public Opinion and Communication.* 2nd ed. New York: Free Press of Glencoe, Inc., 1953.

Brim, Orville G., Jr. *Sociology and the Field of Education.* New York: The Russell Sage Foundation, 1958.

Burgess, E.W., and Donald J. Bogue (eds.). *Contributions to Urban Sociology.* Chicago: The University of Chicago Press, 1964.

Clausen, John A. *Sociology and the Field of Mental Health.* New York: The Russell Sage Foundation, 1956.

Clift, Virgil A., *et al* (eds.). *Negro Education in America: Its Adequacy, Problems, and Needs.* New York: Sixteenth Yearbook of the John Dewey Society, 1962.

Janowitz, Morris. *Sociology and the Military Establishment.* New York: The Russell Sage Foundation, 1959.

Kirkpatrick, Clifford. *The Family: As Process and Institution.* 2nd ed. New Ronald Press Co., 1963.

Miller, Delbert, and William H. Form. *Industrial Sociology.* 2nd ed. New York: Huber, 1964.

Ohlin, Lloyd E. *Sociology and the Field of Corrections.* New York: The Russell Sage Foundation, 1956.

Rose, Arnold M., and Caroline B. Rose (eds.). *Minority Problems.* New York: Harper & Row, Publishers, 1965.

SOME OF THE LEADING GENERAL SOCIOLOGICAL TEXTS

Broom, Leonard, and Philip Selznick. *Sociology.* 3rd ed. New York: Harper & Row, Publishers, 1963.

Chinoy, Ely. *Sociology.* 2nd ed. Evanston, Illinois: Harper & Row, Publishers, 1958.

Rose, Arnold M. *Sociology.* 2nd ed. New York: Alfred A. Knopf, Inc., 1965.

Index

Index